JEAN-PAUL SARTRE

Modern Literature Monographs

JEAN-PAUL SARTRE

Liselotte Richter

Translated by Fred D. Wieck

Frederick Ungar Publishing Co.
New York

Published by special arrangement with Colloquium Verlag,
Berlin, publishers of the original German

Contents

1   *Alienation and Justification:*
Roots of Creativity   1

2   *The Principal Themes of Sartre's Thought*   23

3   *Resistance: Freedom and Responsibility*   55

4   *Dialogue with Friend and Foe*   77

5   *Liquidation of the Past—*
Not a Faith for the Future   105

     Chronology   111

     Notes   115

710036

All dates given in the text, whether for French originals or their English titles, refer to the first French publication.

1

Alienation
and Justification:
Roots of Creativity

It is characteristic of every philosophy of existence that in order to understand it we must pay close attention to the specific circumstances in which its author's existence is inextricably involved. This is especially true of the philosophy of Jean-Paul Sartre, the author of existentialism in the strict sense of the word. Let us look, then, at Sartre's face, in a state of intense mental concentration: the somewhat unhappy and tormented expression, the furrowed forehead, the stubborn set of his mouth, his absent-minded right eye straying outward behind its thick lens. There is about it all an aura of exhaustion, of homelessness and alienation—the alienation of a lost or abandoned child who finds himself exposed to nature and history and there left at the mercy of a chaos to which he must now, all alone, give meaning through superhuman work and concentration. Alone and single-handedly he must create an absolutely original design, a bold, unprecedented project of his life as a person, as an artist, and as a thinker.

As such an individual sees life, every man finds himself forever on a dreadful proscenium of freedom, the freedom to which all men are condemned. Man is forever the absolutely free dramatist staging the drama of his own life. Sartre himself described it:

We have our problems—the problems of ends and means, of the just use of power, the consequences of our actions, the relation of the individual to the community, the individual's action within the historical context, and hundreds of other questions. It seems to me that the dramatist's task is to make his choice among life's borderline situations and to choose that one which best expresses his concern, and to present it to the public as the question that is posed to freedom.

The profound inner discord that lies behind all this—the unhappy sense of living a life of total abandonment, in the enervating awareness of being forever on stage, watched by a thousand eyes and forever compelled to make decisions—this is the all-too-clear-eyed vision of a solitary, forlorn conscience. In Sartre's view, all men are disinherited outcasts, vile cowards, and traitors. Every conscience in the world is, at this moment in history, abandoned to its own solitude. Every man who is concerned with his own freedom and the authenticity of his "project of living" is not just acting like an overly scrupulous philosophy professor. Think of the Negroes, the Jews, the poor, the North Africans. Their desperate situation reflects the tragic conflict in the life of every man.

Sartre spoke of all men as "bastards and traitors." Bastards, because we all lead double lives—one life legitimate, the other illegitimate—a collective community of oppressed and humiliated beings who must forever justify their own existence. Traitors, because we never make an absolutely free decision, but are slaves of the human condition which casts us into a concrete situation, because everything we are and do is always determined by *mauvaise foi* (bad faith), which poisons every second of our lives. Every one of us is just like the colored peoples who are caught between two cul-

tures and thus must live in perpetual alienation—
aliens either to their own culture or to the culture
forced on them from outside.] The situation of the
proletarians in the class struggle is analogous.

This consciousness of alienation, the consciousness of being an outcast and (as Hegel had
said long ago about the proletarians) dehumanized
is not just a histrionic pose with Sartre or an ab-
struse problem for intellectuals. This consciousness
arises from the very roots of Sartre's own life.

Sartre was born on June 21, 1905. Before
reaching the age of two, in 1907, he lost his father,
an officer in the French navy, who was killed far
from home, in the East. His widowed mother re-
turned to her parents' home in La Rochelle. She
did not remarry until ten years later. To all ap-
pearances, Jean-Paul was a happy child, the darling
of his grandfather who plied him early with diffi-
cult questions. The child would often answer them
in such original and startling ways that the old man
would exclaim: *"Voilà un type extraordinaire!"*
Future events were to reveal just how extraordinary an individual he was.

But Sartre's grandfather, though revered by the
child as an authority, could not replace his father.
Looking back on his fatherless childhood, Sartre
spoke of himself as a *faux bâtard* (a false bastard).
Despite the fact that he was of legitimate birth and
fully accepted by his family, he never thought of his
existence as justified in any way. The behavior of
all these grown-ups who admitted him to their

circle, spoiled him, and offered him explicit proof
that he had a rightful place in the world early impressed the boy as forced, overdone—the poses of
playactors. "My grandfather," he said, "was a great
playactor (a clergyman!), and so was I—all children are, more or less. Everything seems just a play
which gradually dominates life more and more."
Jean-Paul sensed that he occupied a privileged
place in a world that idolized him—sensed it so
clearly that his precocious mind could not fail to
know that he was, in fact, displaced. This is the reason why he strove forever to "justify" his existence.

The revelation of his youth continues: "I
never came to know the feeling of *property*. Nothing ever was my own, because first I lived with my
grandparents and then, after my mother's remarriage, I could still less feel at home with my step-
father. It was always 'the others' who gave me what
I needed."

The feeling of being homeless and without
possessions—a feeling he shared with the poor and
with all those who lived on life's dark side—was
thus a part of his earliest and most basic experiences. This feeling, of being penniless, also moved
him to reject the generosity of Simone Weil, who
gave all her earnings to the poor. Such generosity,
he felt, was basically a feudalistic phenomenon, reflecting, as he said, "a freedom broken by feudal-
ism. Don't talk to me about 'selflessness' and 'sanc-
tity.' She simply thought that the money did not

belong to her, because she regarded the present wage system as absurd."

Sartre's own literary generosity, of which he gave ample proof, did not, however, stem from resentment. "I owned nothing," he said, "but I never suffered from it." What made him suffer was not that he accepted gifts—he suffered because he himself was *too much* accepted. Being excessively accepted in the adult world threw him back, he felt, upon his own totally unjustifiable existence. "What I have," he said, "does basically not belong to me—it is alien to me." He did not want his generosity to be confused with the degrading form of feudal or bourgeois generosity. The trauma of losing his father was the true source of his persistent feeling that he was a proletarian, someone who had to justify his existence. Thus we are told by his friend and fellow fighter Francis Jeanson.

We have seen, then, how the seemingly happy, simple, and well-ordered life of his childhood soon became enormously complicated and divided against itself. His own existence, and everything connected with it, appeared to him ambiguous and questionable. Everything conspired to make him regard the situation of the *homme aliéné*—the alienated man—as his own, most personal problem. A passionate will to offer self-justification, and to achieve a justice that would be measured by other than average standards, developed early in him and has stayed with him throughout his life. In this light we must interpret a statement he made at a press conference held on his return from a journey to South America late in November, 1960: "I demand to be accused, just like my fellow fighters who also signed the *Declaration of the 121*." Official arraignment before a court was not to be withheld from him, he declared.

In the bohemian surroundings of Madame de Beauvoir's studio, cluttered with books, toiletries, South American folk art and samurai swords, the participants in the press conference—most of them seated on the floor—became involved in a debate about Algiers. Sartre offered the following comment. The *Declaration of the 121* was not, he said, a call to disobedience, but merely a declaration of solidarity with those who had taken upon themselves the decision to disobey: "By taking the stand we took, we give a possibility of free decision to the young people who are exposed to constant influences from all sides, and whose minds are being raped today. The rape consists in this, that they are being exposed to demoralization by a war which includes torture and assassination in its very structure."

What mattered to Sartre here was justice, and also freedom—the freedom to make one's own decisions in life. Let us note, at the same time, that Sartre thought of himself as being upon a large stage, before the eyes of the great public. From childhood up, Sartre had been conscious that life, which his environment tried to offer him in such abundance, was actually being withheld from him.

How could such a comedy, such mutual masquer-
ading, be justified? How can we penetrate to the
actual truth behind it? When he was barely eight or
nine years old, Sartre had written "novels" in the
attempt to answer this question for himself, by
means of stories still strongly influenced by the
children's books he was then reading. As early as
the age of four or five, impressed by La Fontaine's
Fables, he had begun to write fables of his own. His
daily life, and his dealings with the adult world,
demanded to be supplemented by his imagination
which called for clearer, less ambiguous situations
than his questionable relations with the adult
world offered. His grandfather's voice impressed
him as all-powerful—and yet, as a comedian's voice
with its excess of cordial good nature. Grandfather,
the only man in the family, bore all the earmarks of
a playactor. This existence—was it not absurd?
And yet, was not this masquerade the one and only
way to hide that absurdity? Grandfather was a professor, and wrote books. Accordingly, the little Jean-
Paul felt compelled to become a professor, so that
he, too, could write books. The situation parallels
that of young Kierkegaard living with his aged,
grandfatherly father. And curiously, Sartre asked
himself the same question—*"Am I Abraham?"*—
which had assumed such central importance for
Kierkegaard, and had compelled him to sacrifice
what was dearest to him, his beloved fiancée.

 Both Kierkegaard and Sartre resorted to literature in their effort to show the seriousness of exist-

ence more clearly than could be done in real life that is steeped in hypocrisy. Both of them opposed dishonest "seriousness" with the idea of the "game" —though the rules of the game differed greatly. For Kierkegaard, they were absolute transcendence; for Sartre, absolute immanence. But for both, the immediate, great justification of their existence lies in the book that they must write. Kierkegaard would write the eternal dialogue with the fiancée whom he had rejected, sacrificed to God's call. (On the day of his engagement, he wrote in his diary: ". . . or: are the orders 'FURTHER'?")

But Sartre, in contrast to Kierkegaard, did not consider the realm of aesthetics as a paradigm of the religious realm. He rejected, and indeed passionately denied, all transcendence, perhaps in reaction to the traumatic experience of his grandfather, a comedian and pastor. His mind was firmly fixed on man's existence hopelessly lost within pure immanence, and totally debarred from any justification in a world beyond. As Roquentin, the hero of Sartre's book *Nausea*, expresses it:

A book. Naturally . . . it wouldn't stop me from existing or feeling that I exist. But the time would come when the book would be written, when it would be behind me, and I think that a little of its clarity would fall over my past. Then, perhaps, because of it, I could remember my life without repugnance. . . . And I might succeed—in the past, nothing but the past—in accepting myself.[1]

The passage could almost have come from the diaries of Kierkegaard—but how great a difference there is in the conclusions Sartre draws! He gives a justification of a homosexual; and he deliberately stops on the level of aesthetics—the level which Kierkegaard considered the lowest level which must be overcome absolutely by a transcendence to the religious level. Sartre knew only the total absence of transcendence—existence caught in the absurdity of this world. Yet Sartre, too, employed the word *existence* as a central concept, which he owed to the religious impetus of Kierkegaard who, like Sartre himself, had early come to consider the dubious nature of bourgeois life an unbearable torment. We shall return to the matter later and trace the causes that prompted Sartre's radical break with the original meaning of existence in transcendence, and made him escape into pure, godless immanence. (Heidegger still says that "to exist means to transcend," though, in a sense, his meaning is quite different from Kierkegaard's.)

Literature as a Substitute for Religion

It is indicative of Sartre's early background that literature came to be for him equivalent to religion. The bourgeois setting of his youth had served to exalt literature in his mind to the level of a veritable priesthood. By such standards, the servant of the spirit rises above the accidents of life; literature atones for the horrors of reality and frees man from the boredom and nausea of existence, while nature is hateful, shapeless, and vague, and has to be tamed by art. Thus Sartre reports that his generation discovered the cinema as a revolt against the adult world: "We went to the movies," he writes, "*against* our families. There I was struck by the difference between the pictures on the screen and actual landscapes. The 'vagueness' of actual landscapes as compared with those on the screen mirrored for me the vagueness of my life—considered, that is, apart from literary works."

Sartre, then, overcame the nausea and surfeit (*ennui*) of the aesthetic stage not by way of religion, but once again by capturing life in aesthetic formulation—in literature. Literature was his substitute for religion because it subjugated the nauseating wildness and vagueness of reality. Here we must seek the sources of his atheism:

There was daily life which was absurd and forlorn. One lived along any which way, merely trying to have the largest possible number of experiences. And beside it, there was the other life to which one could gain access by writing, by creating a book. Literary acts possessed a metaphysical value, they were inscribed in some sort of Absolute—but it was a laicized Absolute, because the point was to make the other world, the world beyond, enter into this world.

Or:

Literature was for me, first of all, the search for justification in the future, the transposition of eternal life; one accepts an accidental and vague existence, in the present, in order to be recognized by human society after one's death. . . .

By the time he was eleven years old, Sartre had ceased altogether to believe in God. (His grandfather was a Protestant, his mother Catholic.) But even though God was dead, "theological things went on." To Sartre, "theological things" referred to an absolute in order to provide a basis for what was merely relative—in short, to render relative matters serious.

We may regard Sartre's grandfather as the "superannuated God" (insofar as he took the father's place in Sartre's father complex). We may also regard him, the professor, as the priest of literature, which was a sort of substitute religion; and in his personal conduct, we may see him as the playactor. From this complex basic experience of the father principle, Sartre derived his authority to continue in all three roles, in his own way, even though he knew perfectly well that he had received no explicit mandate. "I work as if compelled by the highest duty," he said, "even though no one has commanded me."

Throughout, his fundamental theme has continued to be the Absolute. What he was searching for in his work was not a mere escape into the aesthetic realm; he was also striving for a morality of salvation—a conversion, as it were, and an advance to a new level. His work, in turn, was to affect life itself. Thus he strove for deliverance from the contingent and vague character of life through contact with Being—Being which is grasped intuitively in work, and overcomes the eternal flux and transiency of things. Ever since entering the *Ecole Normale* in 1924, Sartre had tried to find a relation to Being in every phenomenon seized by his mind—to find the presence of the Absolute in what is merely relative. He was convinced that man becomes truly man only by overcoming the relative situation of human existence. It took him more than fifteen years, until the time of *Nausea*, to conquer this "theological" need for transcendence within himself. "I have searched a long time for the Absolute," he said. In fact, he never overcame that need altogether. He merely transposed it more and more into worldliness and immanence. He absorbed transcendence and eschatology into immanence, so to speak—the tragic error of all programs of universal happiness and all Utopias, an error which is fruitful and frightful at the same time.

In the same area, we must seek the explanation of the mysterious fact that even in the heat of the class struggle, which repeatedly absorbed Sartre's energies, he could never quite subordinate literature to politics. All he could do was to place the two in a dialectical relationship. He could make his peace neither with a literature of political propaganda nor with pure, uncommitted literature. Such one-sided attitudes were to him a betrayal both of literature and of the idea of revolution. "The art of writing," he wrote, "is not protected by the unalterable decrees of Providence; men make it, men choose it, by choosing themselves. If this art were to change into pure propaganda or into pure pleasure, mankind would relapse into the mire of immediacy. . . ." He called for a *littérature engagé*, a "total literature," the "total expression of the human situation." Such a literature aims to show man to himself as a totality that is responsible for everything. "Every man is all men," he expressed it, "every human undertaking, however isolated it may seem, involves all mankind." And again: "Every suffering of whatever kind is always also the totality of all suffering."*

This earnest will to achieve the Absolute places Sartre very close to the pathos of the religious realm, even though he is an atheist. Again, we must not allow him to mislead us. We must understand Sartre's atheism in terms of its origin. The will to the Absolute has remained. In 1945, Sartre declared that the issue was not that of talking about the existence of God, and that even if God did exist nothing would be changed for man: "It is necessary for man to find himself, and to realize that nothing can save him from himself."

Sartre's atheism, then, must be understood dialectically; here, once again, we encounter the paradox of a love-hate whose ambivalence will incline now in this, now in the opposite, direction. Nothing is ever final here. We must be prepared for the most absurd leaps, and indeed, must be ready to perform such leaps ourselves. Sartre denies God, so to speak, only in the forefront of his consciousness, as a *modus deficiens*—as a privation, not a negation. We must never lose sight of that orig-

* See also page 100.

inal situation in Sartre's life story from which his attitude arose: he loved what he denied, because it was what he had missed most profoundly when he was a child who had no father—a child who had been made suspicious by the consolations of over-zealous adults, and had turned into a subtle and tricky disputant.

Even in his attitude toward the ultimate questions, Sartre, with his will to the Absolute, proceeded from a mandate that no one gave him. "It was the result," he said, "of my *tradition humaine*," he said, "and I had to live in this contradiction with myself." Deeply within him, he admitted, there was a certain ultimate, a "certain personal evidence that could not be defied." We shall now trace this last remark to its roots, by following the development of his work.

Sophistic Revolt

By now we have learned a good deal of the roots of Sartre's convictions: his world without transcendence, his concern with man alone, his rejection of the cosmos. The great themes of mankind, such as they present themselves in the history of philosophy, appear in Sartre's work only sporadically. The archaic cosmogony of awakening childhood is lacking altogether—indeed, he has no feeling at all for children. They hardly ever play a part in his novels, and if they do appear they are in fact merely small adults. Sartre's world is made up wholly of adult problems; nature with its flowers, animals, and landscapes does not interest him. His total lack of understanding for animals is shown, for instance, in the torturing of the cat in *The Age of Reason*. He deals with his poor animals as though they were evil adult human beings who vent their malice without inhibitions. In a similar vein, we read of the young fellow in *The Reprieve* (sometimes called Pablo, sometimes Pedro: "Little Pedro looked at him earnestly . . . behind the confused moods that glittered in his eyes, a small and greedy awareness was lying in ambush . . . 'And that thing thinks!' Mathieu said to himself."

Sartre's universe is all rational consciousness, as we meet it in man's ego-consciousness phase during the defiant period of puberty. If Sartre mentions landscape at all in his work, it is only as the reflection or the object of his consciousness. He declines to value nature as an independent being, in the pan-psychic or mystical sense. This attitude, too, constitutes one of the roots of his atheism. It is impossible for him to speak of God, except as the object of a fully aware adult modern consciousness. And since such a consciousness cannot grasp and define God, He does not exist for Sartre. This limitation, which confines Sartre to the world of mature adults, is highlighted by a remark of his life-long companion, Simone de Beauvoir, in the second volume of her autobiography: "A child," she writes, "would not have tied the bond between us any more closely . . . to bear children is to augment the number of children on earth vainly and without justification. . . ."

Equally striking is Sartre's almost exclusive interest in the social and psychological aspects of life. Simone de Beauvoir, telling of walking tours through the Provence (she covered up to twenty miles a day), does reveal an eye for the beauties of the landscape—but she never says one word about stopping for a rest, or of self-oblivion through becoming absorbed in nature.

The sophistic revolt of ego-consciousness in the youthful phase—the conflict between subject and object—was, on the other hand, something that Sartre consciously seized upon as his own problem, a problem he has had to overcome by means of the epistemological subject-object dialectics of his mature work—in Phase 3, so to speak, in the evolution of mankind. *"Reconcilier l'objet et le sujet!"* he demanded—and thereby he turned the Marxist interpretation of life into a relative matter. Here again he himself personifies the paradox of the sheltered son of a middle-class home, who is at the same time convinced that he is disinherited, a proletarian, and who is striving to justify his own existence: "a common human being, resembling everyone and no one," who did not feel "at home" (*chez soi*) anywhere. This is the voice of the precocious revolt of puberty, the sophistry at odds with the object. It is an echo of the words of Protagoras that "man is the measure of all things—things in being

because they are, and things not in being because
they are not."

In Heidegger's *Being and Time,* the philo-
sophic center is the world of Being exclusively, all
else being merely things that are at hand and available, things that are tools. Sartre wanted to go still
further and eliminate the objective world altogether. In the typical conflict between subject and
object, he consciously sided with the subject. He
did so even in his earliest works, *Imagination* and
The Psychology of Imagination, and still more pro-
nouncedly in *Being and Nothingness.* Existence as
the human manner of being, the essential being,
was consciously opposed to the being of mere objects. Thus he wrote in *Action,* December 29, 1944:

Have you ever defined existentialism for your readers? It's so
simple! In philosophical parlance, every object has essence
and existence. An essence (inherent nature) means a constant whole of properties (*un ensemble constant de pro-
priétés*); an existence (being) means a certain effective presence in the world. Many people believe that essence comes
first and existence later: for instance, that the young peas
grow and become round by corresponding to the idea of
young peas, and that cucumbers are cucumbers because they
share in the idea of cucumber. This notion has its origin in
religious thought. True, anyone who wants to build a house
must first know exactly what kind of an object he wants to
make: essence comes before existence; and all those who believe that God made man must believe also that He did so by
referring to the idea He had of man. But those who do not
share this belief have nonetheless retained the traditional
view that the object has existence only in its agreement with
its essence . . . Existentialism, on the other hand, asserts

that in man—and in man alone—existence precedes essence.
This simply means that man first of all *is*, and only subsequently is this or that particular man. In a word, man must
create his own essence for himself; he defines himself gradually by casting himself into the world, by suffering and
struggling in the world; and *the definition remains forever
open.* . . . Accordingly, is existentialism fascist, conserva-
tive, communist, or democratic? The question is absurd. On
this level of generality, existentialism is nothing at all except
a certain way of approaching human problems which refuses
to assign to man a mode of being that is fixed forever.

What is basic here is the distinction Sartre
makes between a "serious" attitude and the freedom of play:

It is serious to begin with the world and to ascribe to the
world more reality than to oneself, and especially to ascribe
to oneself a reality in proportion as one belongs to the world.
. . . All serious thinking has achieved its density through
the world. It congeals; it is an abdication of human reality in
favor of the world. The serious man is "world," and is no
longer sustained within himself; he does not even any longer
consider the possibility of leaving the world behind, because
he has given himself the type of existence of a rock—its con-
sistency, inertia, being-in-the-world. It goes without saying
that the serious man has buried the consciousness of his freedom in his own depths. He is insincere (*de mauvaise foi*),
and his insincerity aims at making him appear, in his own
eyes, as a conclusion: to him, everything is consequent, and
there is no principle ever; this is why he gives so much attention to the consequences of his actions. . . . Man is serious
when he takes himself for an object.[2]

Man in the Subject-Object Split

In the passage just cited, the essential motifs are those of the opposition of object and subject, of world and ego, and of flight into seriousness as a flight from the freedom of one's own subjectivity. The precedence of existence over essence here, too, has its concrete basis. If essence—the Idea—were primary, then man's existence would be merely the consequence of a principle not of his own making. To give precedence to existence—to being—over idea means that man, instead of relying upon laws given in the nature of things, must begin his own existence freely—as if it were a game—and must himself establish the rules of the game from the very start. In this way man himself is the source of his own existence, and the creator and master of a game he himself has invented. His existence is not without law; it is not arbitrary. It follows a law which he himself has established.

In addition, we have just come across an expression that will be basic to our further study of Sartre's thought—the expression *"mauvaise foi."* We add another passage to define its meaning more fully: "As soon as man conceives himself as free and wants to use his freedom, his activity is play, a game, however great his anguish may be. He is indeed the first principle of that game. He himself establishes the value and the rules of his actions, and is ready to pay off only according to the rules that he himself has set up and defined. . . ." [3]

Man lives a split life and is not always aware of his double life—perhaps because he does not want to become aware of it. According to Sartre, man wants freedom as the pure project of existence, but his dread of this absolute freedom makes him flee into the world of objects—a world he rejects because, basically, he is striving for the ideal of freedom. Sartre adopted Kierkegaard's famous definition "Dread is the vertigo of freedom" as it had been adopted before him by the existential philosophers who were to become his teachers; but Sartre stripped it of its original religious meaning. This process of secularization was itself perhaps a half-unconscious *mauvaise foi*. It may well be one of the weak points that could be the starting point of a careful critique of existentialism.

Mauvaise foi is crucial to any understanding of Sartre's philosophy. It is the key not only to his philosophical works but to his novels, stories, and plays as well. Reading his novels, which torment us with their crescendo of repulsive events and characters, we are forced to ask ourselves: What is the purpose of this mysterious method and its destructive, depressing, negative ways? The answer is that Sartre wants to exhibit the infinite variety of actual man as the embodiment of *mauvaise foi*, of bad faith and self-deception, in order to reveal to man the roots of his own existence. By putting his finger on the wound of "mauvaise foi" he wants to help modern man escape from his inner discord.

It was of the essence of human consciousness at

the dawn of mankind to take the cosmos seriously and to feel secure in its keeping—in the sense of the pre-Socratic *sympatheia ton holon*, the *sympnoia panta*, "all things breathing in one." Even so, the Stoics claimed that individual, sinful man had fallen from this harmony and had to be healed according to their guiding principle, *homologoumenos to physei zen*—by living in keeping with the *logos,* the divine law, the *physis,* the living and growing cosmos!

But for Sartre, that original security no longer exists. His sense of being illegitimate and living life illegitimately became expanded in philosophical and poetic terms into the experience of the absurd. God the Creator was no longer a reality for Sartre. In the same way, the awareness of a total "dis-creation" (*décréation*) took hold of his entire generation. Absurdities in nature and history; chaos, dread, nothingness, and nausea; the splitting apart of essence and existence, subject and object; contempt for, and suppression of, the object as nauseating, in favor of the subject; the superman who wants to be *ens causa sui,* that is, wants to be God: all this led up to Sartre's outcry: Man is a "useless passion"—or, as he later on expressed it more crudely: Man is a "common marmalade." How he came to coin this curious expression will be shown briefly in the reflections that follow, when we come to analyze his book *Being and Nothingness,* from which the foregoing passages have been quoted.

2

The Principal Themes of Sartre's Thought

Man existing in free self-determination is, so to speak, no more than an ideal, a model which never occurs in reality. The men who do occur in reality are a very specific mixture (a marmalade!) of freedom and the lack of freedom, of being a subject and being an object. They are forever fleeing, fleeing from the dread of freedom and into the seriousness of the objective world. In the section of *Being and Nothingness* explicitly entitled "Ethical Implications," Sartre wrote:

> . . . the principal result of existential psychoanalysis must be to make us repudiate the *spirit of seriousness*. . . . We are already on the moral plane but concurrently on that of bad faith (*mauvaise foi*), for it is an ethics which is ashamed of itself and does not dare speak its name. It has obscured all its goals, in order to free itself from anguish. Man pursues being blindly by hiding from himself the free project which is this pursuit. He makes himself such that he is *waited for* by all the tasks placed along his way. Objects are mute demands, and he is nothing in himself but the passive obedience to these demands.
>
> Existential psychoanalysis is going to reveal to man the real goal of his pursuit, which is being as a synthetic fusion of the in-itself with the for-itself; existential psychoanalysis is going to acquaint man with his passion." [1]

Mauvaise foi, then, is the intermingling within a single human existence of two different value systems—the demands of the absolute ideal of the project of existence as a pure game, and the concrete existence which is always a flight into seriousness and objectivity. To express this split and discord within man, Sartre employed two

24

Hegelian terms, "in-itself" and "for-itself," whose meaning in Sartre's writings will be discussed in the next chapter. Sartre's essential point was that this split makes evident once again the basic meaning of the word "existence"—a word derived from *ec-sistere*, to step outside of oneself, out into being in the world, and thus enter into a dichotomy, a doubling of the self. This dichotomy of the "in-itself" and "for-itself" is what he had in mind when he spoke of that "synthetic fusion" for which man is striving passionately. A further quotation will make its fundamental meaning clear:

Every human reality is a passion in that it projects losing itself so as to found being and by the same stroke to constitute the in-itself which escapes contingency by being its own foundation, the *ens causa sui*, which religions call God. Thus the passion of man is the reverse of that of Christ, for man loses himself as man in order that God may be born. But the idea of God is contradictory and we lose ourselves in vain. Man is a useless passion.[2]

This (far from unique) reference to God as an "absolute construction" reveals a curious inner contradiction in Sartre's philosophy. Sartre the atheist, with his recurrent variations on the statement: "The project of human reality is man projecting to be God," introduced the concept of God even though Sartre the philosopher, according to his own philosophy, should manage strictly without it. This fact—to which we could add others—permits us the fundamental realization that Sartre himself suffered from *mauvaise foi*. Measured critically by his own philosophical standards, Sartre is the embodiment of that split in two (*dedoublement*) of man which his philosophy seeks to overcome.

The impetus of Sartre's philosophical endeavor to overcome *mauvaise foi* stems from the fact that he himself is greatly suffering from it. All his accusations, all his attacks, all the shrill tones that he favors in his philosophical as well as his creative works are, in a way, the generalized, outward projection of his own inner discord—the dramatization of his self-criticism. It must be admitted, of course, that a man who has become conscious of his *mauvaise foi* is already a step ahead of those who have not yet discovered that situation within themselves. Indeed, Sartre, one of the first modern thinkers to understand these relations, had every right to devote his life to an exposition of this insight, in various didactic and purifying formulations.

Nonetheless, it must be said here that the discovery of *mauvaise foi* is in itself by no means a unique contribution of modern philosophy. The idea had arisen before, at critical turning points in the history of Western thought. At the end of antiquity, for example, we encounter it in the Christian consciousness of St. Paul. In Chapter 7, "Letter to the Romans," Paul revealed the *mauvaise foi* of his era by pointing to the spiritual law that man wants to obey but cannot because he is also subject to the law that courses in his blood. "For the good that I would I do not; but the evil which I would not, that I do." [3]

Again, at the end of the Middle Ages, in the transition to modern times, Luther, struggling in his solitary cell, learned that our will is broken and that we are incapable of the free *facultas faciendi*, because even our *facultas cogitandi* is unfree; that we cannot love God with pure and selfless love, because every action we perform through our own strength is already motivated by selfishness.

More recently, in the dawning sense of crisis that overcame European consciousness in the middle of the nineteenth century, we have Kierkegaard's view of human existence, the view that still sustains all of modern existential philosophy: the insight that if a man truly examines his conscience with complete seriousness, and submits to the absolute demand of the ideal, he can never live up to the goal that is set for him: "Purity of heart is to will one thing only!" The curse of our actual existence is that it is a scattering flight from ourselves—that we are never capable of willing one thing only but always will something else besides. In the transition era from antiquity to the Middle Ages, Augustine, in a similar situation, saw that the human will is never unequivocal, that every action springs from a number of motives, like a tree rising from many roots. And so thought Pascal, in the equally important transition period of the 17th century.

It is clear, then, that Sartre is not unique in the insight he achieved. But one thing distinguishes

him fundamentally from all earlier thinkers—and
that is the laicization of religious motifs of thought,
motifs which formerly could become the source of
deliverance because they drew strength from a
transcendence behind them. This laicization is
characteristic of modern existential philosophy.
Sartre, by constantly stressing his atheism, emphasizes that he intends to stay within the sphere of
immanence. His *mauvaise foi*, at its deepest, is of an
altogether different kind. While it strives to find a
rational immanent clarification as a road to man's
self-liberation, it conceals from itself the fact that,
in order to clarify its own goals, it has had to fall
back, and constantly has fallen back, upon transcendence (Sartre's "Absolute").

This may explain why Sartre's attacks on religious thought and the religious life are so vehe-
ment and vitriolic: His self-observation may have
made him feel the need to extirpate such motiva-
tions within himself. Thus in the scene in his play
The Flies, when a pietistical old woman is shouted
down as an "old slattern," Sartre did not mean only
to denounce religious hypocrisy and the self-deception of conventional religious lip service. Not all
piety, after all, is hypocritical; there is such a thing
as authentic piety. Sartre meant to denounce *himself*. He was not altogether sure of himself. He was
aware of the fractured and disharmonious quality
of modern life, and wanted to use the most radical
means available to fight any illicit recourse to religious symbolism—which even he himself had to

use—in order to achieve the ideal he proclaimed, of an entirely unequivocal philosophy of atheism.

Existentialism, the philosophy that is a cry for existence, stems at bottom from the discovery that we have lost existence within ourselves. This simple statement had found its philosophical formulation in Hegel's dictum that Minerva's owl takes wing only when night is falling. Only when we are no longer sure of our existence, only then do we feel the need to philosophize about it in order to regain it. Christian existentialists since Paul have known that this cannot be done by means of immanence alone, without recourse to transcendence. Modern atheist existentialism subsists on the internal contradiction that, according to its demands, man is to transcend himself by the means of his finiteness.

Sartre's *mauvaise foi*, as we have seen, consists in this, that his philosophy feeds on the very thing that it opposes. Accordingly, a special kind of dialectic has developed in his work. We notice a continuous twisting and turning, a constant partial retraction of his own formulations—something that is hard to describe, because it is so elusive. He himself spoke of the *methode du cercle*, a circular method in which every assumption dissolves again into its opposite. For example, the atheism that is the goal has recourse to the *theos*. The man who wants to confine himself to his own pure subjectivity must be active in the world—that is, he must be serious. Sartre's conclusions often adopted

verbatim the formulations of the mystics, as in "I
am not my being, and my being is not I." Such a
manner of thinking cannot be grasped rationally—
a genuine discussion using such formulations is not
possible. For Sartre can follow every thesis with a
counter-thesis that partially retracts and limits it.

"The Chips Are Down"

In this light, too, we must understand the
curious contradiction in Sartre's doctrine of freedom. I freely choose only myself, he asserts, I alone
establish the rules of the game of my existence; but
in this choice I also want to choose all humanity
and to share in its determination—and all this despite my explicit denial of the precedence of essence, of the essential idea. Thus I may not, by virtue of my choice, impose an essential idea on another person; I must allow him the free decision to
establish his own rules. Here Sartre invokes Hegel's
remark, "If all men are not free, no man is free."
The same holds true of existential freedom which,
Sartre himself has had to admit, is not a complete
freedom from all situational ties. In this sense
Sartre has spoken explicitly of the paradox of freedom. "It is the paradox of freedom," he wrote,
"that freedom exists only in the situation, and situation exists only in freedom."

Sartre thus was unable to carry out his thesis
with that absolute univocity which he had postu-
lated. He encountered the dichotomy of *mauvaise*

foi wherever he turned—and used it brilliantly by making it the method of his philosophical and literary creativity. This method accounts for the scintillating magic of his sentences, and of his fictional characters. Let us look at a concrete example. His most accomplished, most lucid, and also simplest piece of writing significantly has recourse to transcendence. It deals with life after death. It is the script for his film *The Chips Are Down*, unique among film scripts for its philosophical depth and splendor of intellectual content. The action of this drama reveals that, in this life, man is never the creator and free lawmaker of a pure game. Only in death is man absolutely free to undertake the pure project of his existence.

In the world of the dead, which, in Sartre's film, intrudes into this world though it remains invisible to the living, a young workingman meets the young wife of a high official. Under the law of the world of the dead, the two are allowed to return to the world of the living because they were meant for each other but did not meet in their first life. They come back to this life; they now want to realize the free project of their existence which they had planned in the beyond. They want to live their love. But they come into conflict with the situational laws of their erstwhile existence. They fall into the inner discord of *mauvaise foi*, and lose out in the struggle. The young workingman must pursue the objectives of the labor movement to which he belongs from his first life; the young woman, trying to live the life of a workingman's wife, finds herself left alone and is irresistibly drawn into the conflicts of her erstwhile family when she tries to save her sister from an unfaithful husband. The conflict between free will and bondage to the outside world emerges with wonderful clarity. The two leading characters, asked about the motives of their actions, are unable to offer an intelligible answer, because they may not refer to their life in the beyond, which is pure freedom.

Man is a "useless passion," Sartre wrote, because he must will something that is not attainable within immanence; and he can enter into transcendence only through death. As soon as we enter life we can no longer be ourselves, but live by *mauvaise foi*. This realization gives a new and surprising meaning to Goethe's remark that "our whole trick is that we give up existence in order to exist." Deliverance from *mauvaise foi*, with its inevitable inner discord, does not come through philosophy, then, but through death. Freedom, in Sartre's sense, means the obliteration of our concrete existence. *The Chips Are Down* shows clearly that, in Sartre's philosophy, man wants to live as free as the dead, and in death wants to exist like a living man. This inner contradiction constitutes the greatness and the limitation of man's being.

This concrete example will lend life and palpability to our understanding of Sartre's abstract thought structure. We are beginning to understand why nothingness and death are at the center of his philosophy. He developed it not as a mere disciple of Heidegger's *Being and Time*, but in independent and original reflection. Anguish and despair are, for him, the two basic attitudes of existence, because philosophy, in Sartre's sense, seeks absolute freedom; and absolute freedom can be realized only in man's detachment from his situation in the world—in his "annihilation" (*néantisation*).

A Husserlian with a Difference

Starting from Sartre's youthful trauma, his feeling that he was a bastard, we have come to an understanding of the roots and basic motives of Sartre's thinking, his urge to *justify* the sophistic revolt of adult men—the main theme of his work. Our first quick outline of his intellectual career has thus run ahead of the events of his life. But his philosophy and his literary work mutually illumine and explain each other. Accordingly, we must now trace in chronological parallel the development of his thinking both in his literary and his philosophical work. The details of his literary development reveal important and original stages in his thought (especially in regard to his contemporaries) and in the ways in which he modified the teachings of the great philosophers who influenced him.

From 1924 to 1928, Jean-Paul Sartre studied at the *École Normale*, the teacher-training school at the University of Paris, to earn the degree of *agrégé* in 1929. From October 1929 to January 1931, he did military service, at Tours, in the meteorology section. From February 1931 until 1933 he taught at a *lycée* in Le Havre; from 1933 to 1934 at the *Institut Français* in Berlin; from 1934 to 1936 again in Le Havre; from 1936 to 1937 in Laon; from 1937 to 1939 at the *Lycée Pasteur*. From 1939 until 1940 he served in the war. From June 21, 1940 to April 1, 1941, he was a prisoner of war in *Stalag* XII in Trier.

His publications during these years were: in 1936, *Imagination*; in 1937, the novella *The Wall*; in 1938, his great novel *Nausea*, which first brought him public recognition; in 1939, a collection *The Wall and Other Stories*, including "The Wall," "The Room," "Erostratus," "Intimacy," and "The Childhood of a Leader." In the same year appeared the scholarly *The Emotions: Outline of a Theory*, and in 1940 *Psychology of Imagination*. Among the journal articles of this period we note *"La Transcendance de l'ego: Esquisse d'une description phénoménologique"* [4] (in *Recherches philosophiques*, VI, 1936/37) and *"Une Idée fondamentale de la phénoménologie de Husserl: l'Intentionalité"* (in *Nouvelle Revue Française*, vol. 52, January, 1939).

He had also attended Husserl's last seminar-lectures as a student at Freiburg, and passionately welcomed the new method of phenomenology as a deliverance from "empirio-criticism." Thus, in *Imagination*, he explained that Husserl's *Ideas* (1913) had placed both psychology and philosophy upon entirely new foundations, and rendered all earlier literature obsolete. Schelling's remark that philosophy is a "beginning science *par excellence*" applies to Sartre as well. He felt that Husserl had made a new beginning—he had made our intuition of the "intentional directedness toward objects" accessible to subjective mental representation. A new perspective was thus opened up on the subject-object relationship. Imagination, the creator of ideas, had moved into the center of our investigations. Consciousness was essentially this productive and creative power, not a mere reservoir for the storage of impressions. Consciousness was thus wholly *sui generis*. It could not be understood by analogy to the phenomena of natural science. That traditional method would lead to a total misunderstanding of consciousness, whose basic structure is intentionality, the subject's directedness toward objects independently of their existence which, following Descartes' suggestion, is "implied."

With this discovery (which had been made before, in scholasticism, and was noted by Brentano, though in a different sense), Husserl had given greater weight to the objects toward which subjective representation is directed; he had endowed them with the character of independent essences. Husserl was less skeptical than Descartes, whose doubt was itself not all-embracing. In his phenomenological *"epoché"* (*epéchein* = to abstain), Husserl was content to place the world of objects "in parentheses" as regards their real existence. In Husserl's view, the world is "the world for me." I do abstain, of course, from all judgments concerning the world's reality, but at the same time it is always there for me, and my attention is an act directed toward it.

Sartre adopted Husserl's concept of intentionality with passionate enthusiasm—the idea that it is in the nature of consciousness to be intentional, that is, tending toward an object. "Consciousness is always consciousness *of* something," as Husserl put it. Thus Descartes' *ego cogito* is changed to *ego cogito cogitatum*: the object that is thought becomes at once a *factum*, a fact of subjective thought. Whether my thinking is directed toward a present or a future object, a real or potential, beloved or hated object, it is always pointed at an object which is not thinking itself but is conceived as being "outside." Heidegger and Sartre, each in his own way, turned this idea in totally different directions (and in the process rendered essentialism and Platonism still more radically obsolete). What they discovered, as a result, was not consciousness and its intended object, but—Nothingness.

With Sartre, the process went as follows: Husserl's dictum, that intentional consciousness is "the turning of my actual glance *at* something," impressed itself deeply upon Sartre's mind. Consciousness, then, was no longer a vessel filled with lifeless contents, but an act, the "turning toward" something. With Husserl, the difference between perception and imagination emerged as follows: "The centaur itself is obviously nothing psychic; he exists neither in the soul nor in consciousness nor anywhere else; he is in fact 'nothing'; he is all in the imagination, or, more precisely: the experience of the imagination is the imagining *of* a centaur." [5]

Perception, on the other hand, is directed toward something actually present, and clearly differs from turning one's gaze, in imagination, at something that is not there. But this is not what concerned Sartre primarily; he was concerned with imagination. In his book by that title, he wrote about Husserl's passage just quoted: "This is a key passage. The nonexistence of the centaur or of the chimera does not entitle us to reduce them to mere psychic functions. . . . Husserl restored to the centaur, in the very heart of its 'unreality,' its transcendence." [6] All of a sudden, the centaur has transcendence, outside the subject, in "unreality," nothingness; *transcendence* meaning here "transcendence of consciousness." Husserl distinguishes the phenomenological being of transcendent things and the absolute being of immanent things.

For Sartre, the image is no longer content of consciousness, it is no longer in consciousness. It becomes an intentional structure of consciousness that is directed toward a transcendent object. Transcendence means: outside of consciousness. But the ego fares the same way: it no longer remains the "pure ego of consciousness" but is projected outside the self, apparently also as a transcendent object toward which reflecting consciousness directs itself. Sartre's essay *"The Transcendence of the Ego"*

explains that consciousness does not include the
ego either formally or materially, but that the ego
is *"dehors,"* outside of consciousness, in the world
as a being of the world, just like the various egos of
other people. In Husserl the ego is conceived as one
of the structures of absolute, pure consciousness; it
is not more certain, only more intimate, than other
egos. With Sartre, the point is the self-revelation
and self-interpretation of man who is outside himself, his *ec-sistere,* his "stepping outside himself" as
existence. "Man is continuously outside of himself."
In his consciousness, there is nothing but the void
and a movement to slip outside oneself: *un glisse-
ment hors de soi.* Man is fleeing from himself until
he is finally completely beside himself. Thus, in his
essay in the *Nouvelle Revue Française* on intentionality as Husserl's fundamental idea, Sartre
wrote: "If you will imagine that we are rejected
and abandoned by our own nature in an indiffer-
ent, hostile, and refractory world, you will have
grasped the profound meaning of Husserl's discovery." [7]

To Sartre, intentionality had assumed an ex-
plosive character; it had become *éclater vers,* an
outburst in the direction of something. This is his
own definition: *"Connaître, c'est éclater vers. . . ."*
Intentionality had become charged with emotion,
it took the form of love or hate, it was now a way to
rediscover the world by means of sympathy or aver-
sion. "Husserl has restored their terror and their
charm to things," Sartre wrote. Husserl, he felt,

had unlocked new doors of access to the world of the prophets and artists; he had created a new space, a new perspective for dealing with the passions. "Ultimately, everything is *dehors*, outside of us, everything including ourselves, outside in world among the others." All fruitless preoccupation with one's own inner life could thus be overcome.

Imagination and Literary Creation

Thus Sartre did, after all, pass through something like an archaic-magical epoch, philosophy's Phase I—the period concerned with the philosophy of the imagination and invention—after he had made Husserl's thought his own. Indeed, his literary works dating from this period can be understood only in juxtaposition with his philosophical studies; and they, in turn, illuminate his philosophical views of the imagination and invention. In his book on the psychology of the imagination, he presents the act of imagination as magical, an incantation:

It is an incantation destined to produce the object of one's thought, the thing one desires, in a manner that one can take possession of it. In that act there is always something of the imperious and the infantile, a refusal to take distance of difficulties into account. Thus, the very young child acts upon the world from his bed by orders and entreaties. The objects obey these orders of consciousness: they appear.[8]

This imaginative function, too, harbors a means by which to escape from our banishment in the midst of the world; and at the same time it is a step forward in our striving for the Absolute. Imaginary objects are indeed purely our creations; they are only what they are, only what we have made them: they are absolute beings. They act, of course, as an eternal "elsewhere," a constant evasion. But the escape to which they invite us is not just such that it would let us get away from our momentary conviction, our prejudices and little troubles; they offer us an escape from every compulsion of the world which seems to present itself as a negation of "being-in-the-world," as an anti-world.

The power of the imagination, the power of the images, is always a denial of the world, but in a very specific manner; to establish an image means to construct an object at the edge of the totality of what is real; and this, in turn, means to keep reality at arm's length, to free oneself of it—in a word: to deny it. The act of imagination is an alteration of conditions, and appears as "sublimation": consciousness, caught in the snares of this world, evaporates: "It is pure spirit taking revenge of nausea."

No wonder, then, that this artistically productive view of the imagination dominates Sartre's first novel, *Nausea*. The hero of the book, disgusted with small-town life and the petty details of his surroundings, feels the estrangement, the absurdity, the forlornness in all the nonsensical events that stare him in the face. In this revulsion to the world he discovers his own existence. Only in the world of the imagination, which he opposes to the world around him, does he feel "saved"—the word the novel's hero Roquentin exclaims when he hears a singer's voice on a recording. By such escape into an imaginary world, the mind attempts to break out of its captivity within the density of existence. It sublimates itself somewhere else, outside of the world or, rather, in that universe which can be discerned at a distance, on the other side of existence —beyond the canvas of paintings: "With the doges of Tintoretto, with Gozzoli's Florentines, behind the pages of books, with Fabrico del Dongo and Julien Sorel, behind the phonograph records, with the long dry laments of jazz." [9]

Thus *Nausea* ends, unexpectedly, with an imaginary success of Roquentin. Illumined by having listened to a phonograph record, he feels "justified"! And the composer and the singer, too, are "justified"! All of them have escaped existence, have cleansed themselves of the sin of existing. And Roquentin, the pederast, has found his way. He will walk the road of art. What is it that art—for instance, the recording of the Jupiter symphony— represents? Obviously nothing except itself. Art does not refer us somewhere else; it is its own analogue. As is well known, Schopenhauer had compared a melody with a Kantian "thing as such." Sartre wrote:

It does not exist. It is even an annoyance; if I were to get up and rip this record from the table which holds it, if I were to break it in two, I wouldn't reach *it*. It is beyond, always beyond something, a voice, a violin note. Through layers and layers of existence, it veils itself, thin and firm, and when you want to seize it, you find only existents, you butt against existents devoid of sense. It is behind them: I don't even hear it, I hear sounds, vibrations in the air which unveil it. It does not exist because it has nothing superfluous: it is all the rest which, in relation to it, is superfluous. It *is*.[10]

The melody is pure being, unencumbered by any existing object cloaking it. It coincides with its meaning; it has no existence. This is why music frees Roquentin of his nausea, why it is his salvation. "Antoine," it says to him, "I shall teach you fervor." It resists falling into the brutal chaos of existence. Music is the total victory over existence, over the "viscous" slime. When we know of no other way out any longer, when the world presses us to act, we try to change it, to make it undergo a metamorphosis. We try to live, not according to the usual laws but in a magic way.

Sartre called emotion an attitude of incantation. "The compulsion of danger serves as the motive for this intention which brings about magic behavior. I see a wild animal coming toward me. My legs buckle beneath me, my heart beats more feebly, I turn pale, I fall down and swoon. Nothing seems less appropriate than this behavior which exposes me to the danger defenselessly. And yet this behavior is a flight. The swoon is a refuge. Nobody believes that it is a refuge for me, that I am trying to save myself by no longer seeing the wild animal. But I, because I cannot avoid the danger in any normal way, I have denied it, I have annihilated it as far as was within my power. These are the limits of my magical influence upon the world." [11]

But imagination isolates us because it belongs to us alone, it contains only ourselves, its creators. No one can follow us and share in it. This is the tragedy of the experiences of Antoine Roquentin, and of Sartre's story collection *The Wall*. No one can follow the dreamers in those stories—the paranoiac cannot be called back out of his madness. There is a wall between men. The ancient sophists, with their "man the measure" proposition, had the same intuition: Assuming something existed, it would not be knowable to all men—and if it were knowable, it could not be communicated. Consequently, there is only nothingness. Thus Gorgias wrote in a fragment entitled "On Nature, or the Nonexistent."

Sartre's heroes, too, find themselves caught in this atomization and isolation. In his most moving story of this period, "The Room," we are told of the utter failure of a woman who attempts to join her husband in his madness. "Her father says to her: You want to live outside the limits of human nature." And she, moved by love, wants to leave the world of normal people:

I must go back. I never leave him alone so long. She would have to open the door, then stand for a moment on the threshold, trying to accustom her eyes to the shadow and the room would push her back with all its strength. Eve would have to triumph over this resistance and center all the way into the heart of the room. . . . Suddenly she thought with a sort of pride that she had no place anywhere. *Normal people think I belong with them. But I couldn't stay an hour among them. I need to live out there—on the other side of the wall.*[12]

Eve has changed the significance of objects. She has, in Husserl's phrase, "intentioned" them to crystalize in *her* sense. She refuses to see them as they are, and even fears the memory of them:

When he set them down, Eve went and touched them in her turn (she always felt somewhat ridiculous about it). They had become little bits of dead wood again but something vague and incomprehensible stayed in them, something like understanding. *These are* his *things,* she thought. *There is nothing of mine in the room.* She had had a few pieces of furniture before; the mirror and the little inlaid dresser handed down from her grandmother and which Pierre jokingly called *"your* dresser." Pierre had carried them away with him.[13]

Still, despite all good will, the objects resist that new imagination which is functioning only halfway. She nonetheless tries to persuade herself of this partial success. "*Yet,* she told herself with anguish, *it isn't possible for me to see them exactly like him.*" [13] She feels encrusted in the old world, and her body holds her there: "Her body was stiff and taut and hurt her; she felt it too alive, too demanding. *I would like to be invisible and stay here seeing him without his seeing me. He doesn't need me; I am useless in this room.*" [13]

In the paroxysm of her autosuggestion, Eve fathoms the exhaustion caused by her failure. "Eve felt exhausted: *a game,* she thought with remorse;

*it was only a game. I didn't sincerely believe it for
an instant. And all that time he suffered as if it
were real."* [14] Eve can never succeed in rejoining
Pierre: "There is a wall between you and me, but
you are on the other side."

This isolating power of the imagination is
nonetheless indissolubly joined with consciousness.
It is just as absurd to try to conceive of a consciousness that does not imagine as to try to conceive of a
consciousness that cannot perform the *cogito*.[15]
And even if the dream is as inadequate for consciousness itself as is this consciousness for him who
numbly exists, it yet does not cease to project itself
into reality, creeping into transcendence, and de-
termining the significance of things. Without imagination there is no transcendence of consciousness.

Things are never truly what they are, the
spirit roves among them, but it is a spirit which has
come down from the world of the imagination and
brought his phantasma along with him. And we
interpret and poetize the world accordingly. Everyone adds his own nature to nature, everyone tries to
possess the world by wholly personal means, such as
through drunkenness or lechery, as in Sartre's later
novels. Everyone "crystalizes" his world for himself. Thus, to the young man in love, the world, a
landscape, music are different when he is near his
beloved; she is the necessary medium through
which he seizes the world, she is the sun "without
whom things are not what they are." Without her
he wants to see his world destroyed, or better still,

see it reduced to its simple statistical meaning. When the beloved goes away, the universe crumbles into chaos, as we are shown in *Nausea*. To transcend, to understand, to crystalize—this is what gives meaning to the feeling of existence.

Roquentin, hero of *Nausea*, in a famous passage set in a public park, de-crystalizes the world, that is, refuses a crystalization which to the mass of mankind is normal, a habit: the banal world. One crystalizes truly, he says, only by making oneself singular; separate, solitary, gaining a perspective on the world that, by its peculiarity, makes the world unstable. Later, in *Being and Nothingness,*[16] Sartre describes such a crystalization of a smoker's world. Things were of value to him only if he could encounter them while smoking. An effort was needed to cut this symbolic tie. "I persuaded myself that I was not taking anything away from the play at the theater, from the landscape, from the book which I was reading, if I considered them without my pipe."

But here, too, as in the case of transcendence, we rid ourselves of one perspective of the world only to discover instantly another. Man cannot exist in the world without changing it; there is in its depth a necessary lie—the lie of being. Every man is capable of living in the world only by his imagination; every one is the artist making his own world. For the artist, there is a still more intense interpretation of this intentionality of the imagination—a fundamental, transforming intention. The painter "labors at his necessary lie"—he selects it, polishes it, educates it, purifies it, perfects it. He wraps up the universe in a dream. As Baudelaire (to whom Sartre devoted an essay later on) had said: "Above all, the artist must not cease to lie."

It is of interest in this connection to read in Simone de Beauvoir, his life companion, that the two had use for painting and sculpture only insofar as they could associate ideas with them—ideas being *their* points of crystalization. In the Prado, only Murillo and lesser painters deserve mention (but not Velasquez, El Greco, or Goya), and Sartre mentions only Guido Reni(!). Later, however, Sartre inspires Simone with enthusiasm for Grüne-wald's Issenheim altarpeice. This is simply their wholly individual and personal way of placing the accents of their imagination upon the objects.

Writer and Philosopher

We observe, then, that Sartre the thinker and Sartre the literary man work hand in hand, that the philosophical insights gained by the former at once become independent and take literary form, and that, in turn, the philosophical abstractions of Sartre's teachers are at once transformed by Sartre's artistic intentions, "trans-crystalized" in Sartre's sense. Since we are dealing here with the basic elements, the beginnings of all his later philosophy and literary work, we shall summarize the main points of his radically new theory of the imagination from the perspectives that are most significant for the philosophy of existence. Like Husserl, Sartre hopes to arrive at an elemental vision—an eidetic reduction, and associates the power of imagination with the central concept of the image. Among the central properties of the image are:

1. The image is a form of intentional consciousness: I have to gaze at something (*viser*).

2. It cannot be the direct observation of an object but must be quasi-observation, and must contain nothing except what consciousness has introduced.

3. In general, it may not be prompted or determined by objects, but must have sprung out of spontaneous, free consciousness.

4. It must characterize its object not as present, but as absent, nonexistent.

Husserl, in the phenomenological *epoché*, merely refrained from making a judgment concerning the reality of the object. Sartre underlines the object's nonexistent character, and presents the act of imagination under four forms: (1) as nonexistent, or (2) as absent, or (3) as existing elsewhere, or (4) as neutral in respect of the judgment about its existence. According to him, these four acts include in different degrees the whole category of negation.

Here Sartre is consciously at odds with all the analyses, so far, of the phenomenologists who, he believes, had misunderstood the intentional structure of the image, and had derived the image too much from perception. But the image-forming act of imagination is a productive process of spontaneous consciousness, and not a thing that resides within another thing, in consciousness. According to him, consciousness has to be conceived as empty of all images coming from outside. He lays much stress on the unreality and nonexistence of the objects of the imagination. The image of his friend Pierre (an existing man) and of a centaur (nonexistent) are merely two aspects of nothingness. What is imagined exists only in the imagination, and nowhere else. This view is specifically Sartre's own. The second part of *The Psychology of Imagination* stresses the synthesis in the act of imagination of intellectual and emotive elements. "If the image presents itself as the lower limit toward which knowledge tends when it becomes debased, then it also presents itself as the upper limit toward which affectivity tends when it seeks to know itself." [17]

The emotions in the act of imagination transport man back to the magical stage, and produce the image by means of incantation. Our attitude toward such an object differs radically from that toward an existing object. In the face of images, love and hate turn into quasi-love and quasi-hate, and our observation of them is mere quasi-observation. The imagined object is, so to speak, between dream and reality.

Inversion of All Precedent

Thus the traditional view is inverted. Now, perception and consciousness, world and art are dominated by the imagination, and not the other way around. Imagination becomes the primary function of consciousness, its typical expression by which it now is analyzed as freedom (spontaneity) and negation. The object is not a stimulus producing a reaction (Kant's "being affected"), because the object, being nonexistent, has become a thought. Consciousness, thus, is not part of a causal relation; rather, it opens up a relation of meaning. Being free, it rests upon the possibility of withdrawing (*reculer*) from reality and positing the object as nonexistent. "To posit the world and to negate it is one and the same act." The world is transmuted into the unreal and imaginary, the world situation in which I do so is negated, and this product of the imagination, according to Sartre, in turn presents itself at every moment as the meaning of what is real.

Many of these views have found their way into modern drama and into surrealism, into sculpture and poetry. This definition of Sartre changes the work of art, too, into something unreal. "The real is never beautiful, beauty is a value that can be applied only to the mental image, and this means the negation of the world in its essential structure." Now, nausea in the face of the experience of unaesthetic reality becomes the basic experience of

existing man. Sartre thus provides the basis for the
imaginary world view of *ec-sist*ing man, of man
who is beside, outside himself, who has stepped outside his own, voided consciousness, out into nothingness. The novel *Nausea* thus is an expression of
the world view of the period between the wars, just
as Goethe's *Werther* was an expression of the
period of sensibility. This nausea becomes the basic
experience of existence in the famous description
of Roquentin in the *Jardin Public*. Roquentin is
trying, in all kinds of ways, to *justify* his existence.
The book's essential idea is: nothing justifies existence. *L'ennui*, surfeit, boredom covers everything
like a crust.

So I was in the park just now. The roots of the chestnut tree
were sunk into the ground just under my bench. I couldn't
remember it was a root any more. The words had vanished
and with them the significance of things, their methods of
use, and the feeble points of reference which men have
traced on their surface. I was sitting, stooping forward, head
bowed, alone in front of this black, knotty mass, entirely
beastly, which frightened me. Then I had this vision.

It left me breathless. Never, until these last few days,
had I understood the meaning of 'existence.' . . . usually
existence hides itself. It is there, around us, in us, it is *us*, you
can't say two words without mentioning it, but you can never
touch it. When I believed I was thinking about it, I must
believe that I was thinking nothing, my head was empty, or
there was just one word in my head, the word 'to be.' . . . I
was thinking of *belonging*, I was telling myself that the sea
belonged to the class of green objects. . . . If anyone had
asked me what existence was, I would have answered, in good
faith, that it was nothing, simply an empty form which was

added to external things without changing anything in their nature. And then, all of a sudden, there it was, clear as day: existence had suddenly unveiled itself. It had lost the harmless look of an abstract category: it was the very paste of things, this root was kneaded into existence.[18]

> The character of the absurd is inseparably inherent in existence. An absolute senselessness stares at us from all sides, like the muzzles of pistols.

The word "absurdity" is coming to life under my pen; a little while ago, in the garden, I couldn't find it, but neither was I looking for it, I didn't need it: I thought without words, *on* things, *with* things. . . . And without formulating anything clearly, I understood that I had found the key to Existence, the key to my Nauseas, to my own life. In fact, all that I could grasp beyond that returns to this fundamental absurdity. Absurdity: another word; I struggle against words; down there I touched the thing. But I wanted to fix the absolute character of this absurdity here. A movement, an event in the tiny coloured world of men is only relatively absurd: by relation to the accompanying circumstances. . . . But a little while ago I made an experiment with the absolute or the absurd. This root—there was nothing in relation to which it was absurd. Oh, how can I put it in words? Absurd: in relation to the stones, the tufts of yellow grass, the dry mud, the tree, the sky, the green benches. Absurd, irreducible; nothing—not even a profound, secret upheaval of nature—could explain it. Evidently I did not know everything, I had not seen the seeds sprout, or the tree grow. But faced with this great wrinkled paw, neither ignorance nor knowledge was important: the world of explanations and reasons is not the world of existence.[19]

"The absurd," says Roquentin, "cannot be derived, it is irreducible." The statement, "My existence is absurd," simply means that my existence has no logical basis. "Sir, you are superfluous, nothing justifies you." The proof is this: "The world existed before you were born, and went on through history, and it will go on in the same way after you are dead." The rejoinder of the person in question, that his family needed him, is refuted with the question: "But is there any justification for the existence of your family?" Here is again the old core question that has tormented Sartre since his early childhood: How can our existence, and that of others, be *justified*? And here again is the same answer: *Il n'est pas justifiable.*[20] In the play *The Victors*, one of the dying men says: "I am not missing any place, I don't leave a gap. The subways are overcrowded. So are the restaurants. The heads are stuffed to the bursting point with petty worries. I have slipped out of the world, and it has stayed full. Like an egg."

But then our existence is accidental and not necessary, not an eternal verity. Thus we read in *Nausea*:

The essential thing is contingency. I mean that one cannot define existence as necessity. To exist is simply *to be there*; those who exist let themselves be encountered, but you can never deduce anything from them. I believe there are people who have understood this. Only they tried to overcome this contingency by inventing a necessary, causal being. But no necessary being can explain existence: contingency is not a delusion, a probability which can be dissipated; it is the absolute, consequently, the perfect free gift.[21]

Frustration, we would say, pointlessness, superfluousness; thus it becomes understandable when he
continues:

> All is free, this park, this city and myself. When you realize
> that, it turns your heart upside down and everything begins
> to float, as the other evening . . . : here is Nausea; here
> there is what those bastards . . . try to hide from themselves
> with their idea of their rights. But what a poor lie: no one
> has any rights; they are entirely free, like other men, they
> cannot succeed in not feeling superfluous. And in themselves,
> secretly, they are *superfluous*, that is to say, amorphous,
> vague, and sad.[22]

Here, even in this early stage of Sartre's thinking,
the characteristics of existence are indicated: contingency, absurdity, anguish, nausea, pointlessness,
superfluousness, impossible to justify, sad, vague,
amorphous. But there emerges at the same time the
paradox, as we shall see in the sequel, that Sartre
associates with this existence which he has found so
negative: the absolute values of infinite responsibility and freedom.

3

~~◇◇◇◇◇◇◇◇◇◇◇◇◇◇◇◇◇◇◇◇◇◇◇◇◇◇◇◇◇◇◇◇◇◇◇◇◇~~

Resistance:

Freedom

and Responsibility

War and occupation served to bring the fundamental modern experience of existence—nausea, nothingness, absurdity—to the forefront of Sartre's awareness and to dominance in his philosophy, and at the same time added the paradoxical counter-ideas of absolute freedom and responsibility.

But first, a few more facts of Sartre's life and work during this period: After military service and his captivity as prisoner of war, he was, on April 1, 1940, exchanged for civilian laborers, and resumed his teaching post at the *Lycée Pasteur*; from 1942 to 1944, he was professor at the *Lycée Condorcet*, and at the same time active as a writer in the resistance. Beginning in 1945, on an indefinite leave from his teaching post, he made his first visit to the United States, as a journalist; he subsequently traveled widely from his Paris residence, especially in the United States, Africa, Scandinavia, and the Soviet Union.

His writings were: *Being and Nothingness*, 1943; the three-volume work *Les Chemins de la liberté*, consisting of *The Age of Reason, The Reprieve*, and *Troubled Sleep*, 1945; *Existentialism, Anti-Semite and Jew*, and *Descartes*, 1946; *Situations I, What Is Literature?* and *Baudelaire*, 1947; *Situations II*, 1948, *Situations III*, 1949; *Saint Genêt, Actor and Martyr*, 1952; in August of that same year, his *Reply to Albert Camus;* and *Critique de la raison dialectique*, 1960. Plays: *The Flies*, 1943; *No Exit*, 1944; *The Respectful Prostitute*, 1946; *Dirty Hands*, 1948; *The Devil and the*

Good Lord, 1951; *Kean* (adapted from Dumas), 1954, *Nekrassov*, 1956; and *The Condemned of Altona*, 1960. Film scripts: *The Chips Are Down*, 1947; and *In the Mesh*, 1948.

The development of Sartre's basic concepts and insights can be understood only against the background of the resistance movement, which was to become the great test of Sartre's existential project. Thus Sartre in 1944 wrote in *Lettres françaises*, under the heading "Republic of Silence":

We were never more free than under the German occupation. We had lost all rights, starting with the right to express our opinions. We were daily insulted to our faces, and had to accept the insults in silence. We were being deported *en masse* as laborers, Jews, or political prisoners. Everywhere—in the newspapers, on the walls, in the cinemas—we had to look at the dirty and monotonous image of ourselves that our oppressors were trying to impress upon us. And in consequence of all this we were free. Because the Nazi poison infiltrated our very thoughts, every independent thought represented a conquest. Because an all-powerful police tried to force us to keep our mouths shut, every single word achieved the value of a proclamation of principle. Because we were chased like dogs, every gesture of ours assumed the significance of a desperate wager. The often horrible circumstances of our struggle made it possible for us to live that fragmented and unbearable existence which is known as the human condition. . . . A single word was enough to provoke ten or even a hundred arrests. *This total responsibility in total solitude, does it not truly unveil the nature of our freedom?* . . . Thus, in darkness and blood, was founded the strongest of all republics. Every one of its citizens knew what he owed to all, and that nonetheless he could rely only on himself. Every one of them played a historic role in utter solitude,

Every one of them undertook, in resisting the aggressors, to be freely and irrevocably himself. And by choosing himself in his freedom, he chose freedom itself.[1]

This exemplary experience of life under the occupation became the lasting model of existence in general. All the characteristics of existence were henceforth illustrated by means of that model. Solitude, silence, and darkness are in the nature of our existence at the present moment in history. By choosing ourselves in the face of torture, concentration camp, and executioner we have made our choice in total responsibility that reveals the nature of our freedom.

Sartre elaborated this idea in *Existentialism,* using as his example a student who had to choose between two value systems: The formalism of Kant's moral law places us, under the radical responsibility of our own concrete choice, between two alternatives of equal value—a free choice by which we not only make a decision concerning ourselves, but simultaneously also make a decision for all mankind. This causes and at the same time reinforces the profound anguish of our existence in a constant extreme borderline situation, which Sartre sees ineluctably bound up with existence. He does not want it to be understood as merely an exceptional situation: it belongs to the absurdity and historicity of our existence, as he emphasized in detail in *What Is Literature?* The writer today no longer writes summer fiction for people on vacation; for us, vacations are over:

Our public was composed of people of our own kind, who
like us lived in expectation of war and death. For these readers without leisure, incessantly occupied with one single
worry, only one single subject could be sufficient: what we
had to write about was their war, their death. After we had,
in a brutal fashion, become one with history, we were compelled to produce a literature of historicity. But the peculiarity of our position, I believe, lies in this, that war and occupation have thrown us into the melting pot of the world, and
led us to rediscover the Absolute in the midst of the relative.[2]

Once again, the absolute and at the same time
absurd character of our existence breaks through
the stigma of torture. There follows an interesting
discussion of Kafka, and of how far he has prepared
and encouraged that absurdity: his "Seek the unat-
tainable transcendence, the world of grace, when
grace fails to come." Probably, Sartre considers
concentration camp and torture chamber as typical
of the existential situation for this reason, too, that
he himself and all individual things and ultimately
the entire universe have originated by accident, not
of necessity, because they are in vain and superfluous. Since their existence cannot be justified by
anything, their fate, too, must be of the same kind.
Here, too, his entire thinking bears the mark of the
deep trauma of his youth, when he could not justify
his existence, when he was like a poor *bâtard*, an
illegitimate child. Our "historicity" consists in being knocked about by fate from one extreme to another.

During the time of the resistance he also
learned of a poet, Jean Genêt, or Saint Genêt, who

was in jail for repeated burglary and theft. Sartre immediately identified himself with that poet. Saint Genêt's existence was no more illegitimate than is ours, the idea of law is a pretext, at bottom our existence is just as *"injustifiable"* as Saint Genêt's. But the poet is more authentic than we, and simply wanted to safeguard the free project of his existence without regard to conventions. Thus, Sartre dedicated to him his book *Saint Genêt, Actor and Martyr*. The poet is always outside the pale of bourgeois society and its hypocritical *"mauvaise foi,"* its mistaken respect of the community. Saint Genêt meant to shape his whole life, not just his poetry, in accordance with his free imagination, out of *his own* innermost responsibility. Sartre's escapades, too, must always be understood in this light. The ossified legal conventions of the bourgeois world appear to him *"injustifiable"* and unauthentic.

Being and Nothingness

The "No!" with which the resistance had to oppose the oppressors led to an awareness of nothingness—one of the major themes of Sartre's principal work, *Being and Nothingness*, which was written during this period. There is a cartoon showing Sartre as Hamlet, with a skull in his hand, speaking the famous "To be or not to be." Is that what "nothingness" means here? For Sartre, non-being derives from the experience of saying *No:*

The *not*, as an abrupt intuitive discovery, appears as consciousness (of being), consciousness of the *not*. In a word, if being is everywhere, it is not only Nothingness which, as Bergson maintains, is inconceivable; for negation will never be derived from being. The necessary condition for our saying *not* is that non-being be a perpetual presence in us and outside of us, that nothingness haunt being.[3]

Here we clearly discern Sartre's advance from Husserl to Heidegger, whose important role in the rediscovery of nothingness was expressed in his analysis of being in *Being and Time*, and centrally in his Freiburg inaugural address "What Is Metaphysics?" The essential connection between anguish and nothingness also comes to the fore. That of which anguish is in dread is nothingness, and at the same time being-in-the-world as a whole. Nothingness is constitutive of being in a very specific way:

Only on the basis of nothingness's original manifestness can man's existence approach and concern itself with particular beings. But since being is by its nature referred to particular beings which it is not and which are itself, it does as such itself derive from manifest nothingness. To exist means: to be held into nothingness. By holding itself into nothingness, existence already surpasses beings as a whole. This surpassing of particular beings is what we call transcendence. If existence did not fundamentally transcend, which now means, if it did not from the start hold itself out into nothingness, then it could never relate to particular beings, and thus to itself. Without the original manifestness of nothingness, there is no selfhood and no freedom.[4]

Here again, Sartre gives to Heidegger's nothingness a new and original interpretation. In Heidegger, the word "existence" is applied exclusively to human being; similarly, Sartre's discovery of things in existence starts from *all* particular beings (ourselves included), and only secondarily from human existence which alone is of interest to Sartre; for man, and only man, can escape from the prison of being an object, by means of the imagination acting in the free project of his existence and in artistic creation. Analogously, Sartre also reinterprets Heidegger's thoughts about nothingness. Heidegger himself, we recall, had taken up Hegel's statement (which Sartre, too, studied closely as particularly important):

"Pure being and pure nothingness is, thus, the same." (*Science of Logic* I, WW III, 74). This statement of Hegel is correct. Being and nothingness belong together, but not because they, seen in terms of Hegel's concept of thinking, agree in their indeterminacy and immediacy, but because Being itself is in its essential nature finite, and manifests itself only in the transcendence of existence held out into nothingness.[5]

Sartre interprets nothingness in terms of *his* ontology of existence. In his *Psychology of Imagination*, he had already commented with regard to his central concept that "to posit an image is to construct an object on the fringe of the whole of reality, which means therefore to hold the real at a distance, to free oneself from it, in a word, to deny it."[6] On the next page, he illustrates the primary role of nothingness in the imagination by the comparison with an impressionist painter who places himself at a convenient distance from the picture in order to recognize the multitude of small brush strokes as a forest. "The possibility of constructing a whole is given as the primary structure of the act of taking perspective. . . . Thus to posit the world as a world or to 'negate' it is one and the same thing." So far, this could be an illustration of Heidegger's thought. But already the accent is different, and it becomes more pronounced if we recall what Sartre, in *Théorie des emotions*, says about the fear at the encounter with a wild animal: "By swooning, I can annihilate the animal as an object of my consciousness, by extinguishing my entire consciousness in swooning." In this way, according to Sartre, existing man reacts to the encounter with the raw existence of other existences, whether things or men, with a continuous movement of flight.

Our existence is a constant evasion, filled with profound horror and nausea, before the absurdity of the naked, brute existence of objects. This flight is a taking of distance, a leap into nothingness, which frees us in that we negate the naked, raw, brute reality which stares at us senselessly from every side, and assures us of our freedom to project our own existence, to be independent of the essence-scheme of the objects through freedom of the imagination; finally, it is the freedom of choosing ourselves in this or that extreme act flying in the face of the seriousness of objects and respectable society.

This is how Saint Genêt is a hero of freedom, the poet and martyr of his own existence.

Here, fundamentally, we have the large and richly varied theme of Sartre's encompassing literary work during these years. Existing as transcending into nothingness has been translated from the most seriously intended but nonetheless academic presentation of its discoverer Heidegger, into the inescapable shrillness of our historicity—our typical historical situation as the victims of the concentration camps confronting the executioners, the red tape of officialdom, conventional moralizers, and the traditional "churchy" Christians. But it began with the nauseated awakening of Roquentin in the *Jardin Public*, face to face with the absurd tree root and stones; with *existence brute* of all the things that have contingent existence, the existence which to Sartre is unjustifiable, which tortures us and wants to take us captive. This *existant brut*, as Sartre calls any existing being, *la chose*, a thing (including our fellow men who can become *"chosiste"*—thinglike—when they prescribe essentials to us, and who are attacked in plays such as *No Exit* and *The Victors*); *tout ce qui est statistique, massif, invariant, plein*, all "that agrees with itself," Sartre called *"en-soi,"* the *in-itself*, which confronts the open, unaccomplished, nonrigid, free project of authentic existence, of *my* subjective being, the *"pour-soi,"* the *for-itself*:

Finally . . . being-in-itself *is*. This means that being can neither be derived from the possible nor reduced to the necessary. Necessity concerns the connection between ideal propositions but not that of existents. An existing phenomenon can never be derived from another existent *qua* existent. This is what we shall call the *contingency* of being-in-itself. But neither can being-in-itself be derived from a *possibility*. The possible is a structure of the *for-itself*; that is, it belongs to the other region of being. Being-in-itself is never either possible or impossible. It *is*. This is what consciousness expresses in anthropomorphic terms by saying that being is superfluous (*de trop*)—that is, that consciousness absolutely cannot derive being from anything, either from another being, or from a possibility, or from a necessary law. Uncreated, without reason for being, without any connection with another being, being-in-itself is *de trop* for eternity.[7]

Sartre's great discovery is the "look of the other." Just as men turned into stone under the gaze of the Medusa, just so the being-for-itself of man congeals, under the gaze of the other, into being-in-itself. Man becomes an object (for instance, an object of appraisal) of the other. True, he now knows what he, taken objectively, is—but he pays rather dearly for this knowledge, because he now is "taken," unfree, an object with which he can do nothing since he has lost his freedom of action. This situation changes only when he in turn "looks at" the other and makes him an object. Now he is free once more, and must depend on himself alone. Everything human is discussed by Sartre from this point of view: God and world, freedom and slavery, employer and laborer, I and We, love and hate. Sexual desire and caresses provide the starting point for extensive revelations concerning human nature and man's relation to his fellows.

In-itself and For-itself

The human presence of subjects (that which alone is called existence by Heidegger) now has different characteristics from being-in-itself, the being of objects. Human existence is variable, fragile, capricious, does not agree with itself, changes from moment to moment, is the artist of its own metamorphoses, can destroy and re-create itself, carries within it the germ of nothingness, is *"vide au milieu"*—empty in the middle—like an empty flower vase, and can give itself the lie. This human existence, following Pascal, thinks, in existing, *that* it exists; it is a *for-itself, pour-soi* in contrast with the *in-itself*, the *en-soi* of the being of objects. It appears as the necessary condition of nothingness, its fragility is nothing else than a possibility of non-being. This distinction between the *en-soi* of the lifeless object and the *pour-soi* of living human existence became the butt of critical jokes by various philosophers such as Alquié or Gabriel Marcel: My day yesterday, being closed and finished, is an *en-soi*. Is tomorrow, then, a *pour-soi*? Or: I have the grippe—is that an *en-soi* or a *pour-soi*? What is decisive is that Sartre intended to bring out sharply this contrast: free man (*pour-soi*) on the one hand, unfree things on the other. Things that are completed, closed, finished (essence) on the one hand; and on the other hand, man who gives a meaning to these things and who is free to deal with that meaning. And this distinction must always be understood against the richly varied background of *Being and Nothingness*, Sartre's existential psychoanalysis.

Nothingness alone opens the possibility to contrast existing man's *for-itself* from the *in-itself* of finished objects. Man, inasmuch as he is still living, secretes nothingness, so to speak; his consciousness of himself prevents him from agreeing with himself; he feels the inner void that is peculiar to him. When life ends, this nothingness vanishes: the dead man becomes a fullness of being (*plénitude d'être*), a rigid *in-itself*. To Sartre, this process is definitive and irreversible. Thus he writes in his novel *The Reprieve*, published about the same time as *Being and Nothingness*, which describes the delay, the "phony war" preceding World War II:

Dead. His life was there and everywhere, impalpable, complete, as full and hard as an egg, so compact that all the forces in the world could not have introduced an atom into it . . . a vast, motionless, vociferous country fair: shouts, laughter, the whistle of the locomotives, and the shrapnel-burst on May 6, 1917, the savage buzzing in his head when he fell between two trenches . . . his life was a thing adrift, enclosing agonies now motionless . . . and all its intercostal agony, with imperishable little jewels. . . .[8]

Things are outside; human consciousness is the void in the middle, which is formed by its own nothingness. Freedom is the peculiarity of human consciousness in that it secretes its own nothingness, eliminates it; consciousness wraps itself up wholly in this void, it exiles itself and makes itself a prisoner within its freedom, it gains a distance that separates us forever from the universe outside:

Outside. Everything is outside: the trees on the quay, the two houses by the bridge. . . . Inside, nothing, not even a puff of smoke, there is no *inside*, there is nothing. Myself: nothing. I am free, he said to himself, and his mouth was dry. . . . I am nothing; I possess nothing. As inseparable from the world as light, and yet exiled, gliding like light over the surface of stones and water, but nothing can ever grasp me or absorb me. Outside the world, outside the past, outside myself: freedom is exile, and I am condemned to be free.[9]

In ever-new narrative and dramatic situations, Sartre elaborates this tormenting consciousness of being empty. The matter is related to the dread of freedom, which had in essence already been discovered by Kierkegaard with his "concept of anguish": being "suspended above a depth of 70,000 fathoms"; the possibility of sinning, which is in the very nature of freedom; dread and anguish as the "vertigo of freedom" in which freedom collapses and man commits sin because, in falling, he grasps at the nearest possibility. For Sartre, the issue was no longer sin; sin, *mauvaise foi*, would be for him precisely the renunciation of the free project of existence, and thus seriousness with one of the standard labels of traditional morality; for Sartre, the point is this feeling of being outside everything we encounter, be it objects and other human beings.

Sartre and Kierkegaard hold this in common, that, in anguish, freedom puts itself in question. Sartre's man strives and yearns for the eternal peaceful fullness of things, he hopes for an absolute, but that hope is vain. Transcendence is, to Sartre, only the transcendence of consciousness, but even *it* is possible only in the act of the imagination, otherwise we are walled up within an existence that knows no transcendence. No escape from the prison is possible, neither upward to the divine nor sideways to the things around us:

Halfway across the Pont-Neuf he stopped and began to laugh: liberty—I sought it far away; it was so near that I couldn't touch it, that I can't touch it; it is, in fact, myself. I am my own freedom. He had hoped that one day he would be filled with joy, transfixed by a lightning-flash. But there was neither lightning-flash nor joy: only a sense of desolation, a void blurred by its own aspect, an anguish so transparent as to be utterly unseeable.[10]

Man's Double Character

Man, existing in the world as being-for-itself, has a double character, however: he exists also as a material object. He has in himself a *structure brutale* that is at once his expression and his limit; his own body is an "outside." His body is of the innermost concern to him, yet it remains a stranger to him. It can be looked at, touched, just like a tree or a statue, and yet we cannot grasp its essential nature. Even with Kierkegaard, man's deep shock of anguish sprang from the paradox that in the sexual act man is at the same time the most exalted spirit and the most brutal body. Sartre uses these areas as the model case for a merciless analysis revealing the double character of human existence—and does so without the least inhibitions, in a manner often profoundly shocking to our sensibilities. In the sexual act, man experiences himself both as nothingness in his freedom, and simultaneously as matter in his facticity, which indeed always places him in a firm and unalterable situation that limits and in part totally suspends his freedom: man flutters back and forth between the two extremes, nothingness-freedom and matter-facticity-bondage. This unsteadiness constitutes his *viscosité*, the sliminess of human existence.

I am never altogether pure consciousness, says Merleau-Ponty, Sartre's intellectual kinsman, whose books (*Sur la Perception* and *Système du comportement*) develop certain of Husserl's ideas and deal afresh with man's subject-object relation. According to Sartre, man is perpetually in a half-way state between solid and liquid. Sartre describes him with words like *figer* (coagulate), *empâter* (turn into crust), consciousness *s'englue* (gets stuck on birdlime), freedom *s'enlise* (sinks into quicksand); applies to him such adjectives as *poisieux* (smeary), *sucré* (sugar-sticky); and calls him "soft caramel" or "curdling cream." Sartre becomes the philosopher and poet of man's viscosity, his oscillation between *in-itself* and *for-itself*. He wants to bridge the chasm between the in-itself and the for-itself, between reality and consciousness, but at the same time to maintain their complete dualism, as the actual characters do in Sartre's novels and plays.

At one time, the in-itself is the intentional object of the for-itself of freedom; at another time,

Sartre sees the for-itself as body, as facticity, as man's being cast into a situation, as dependent on the in-itself. His monumental 700-page work, *Being and Nothingness,* is a gigantic, Sisyphus-like labor to present the futility of human existence between freedom and objectness—its viscosity; and in his novels and plays he tries to portray man fluttering back and forth between these two extremes. Man, being "brutal structure," is a body which concerns him directly and at the same time remains strange to him. Man can look at his own body as if it were a statue, can touch it without grasping its essential nature. Sartre depicts the experience in *The Reprieve:*

He reached out his hands and slid them slowly over the stone parapet, it was wrinkled and furrowed, like a petrified sponge, and still warm from the afternoon sun. There it lay, vast and massive, enclosing in itself the crushed silence, the compressed shadows that are the insides of objects. There it lay: a plenitude. He longed to clutch to that stone and melt into it, to fill himself with its opaqueness and repose. But it could not help him: it was outside, and forever. There lay his hands on the white parapet: bronze hands, they seemed, as he looked at them. But just because he could look at them, they were no longer his, they were the hands of another, they were outside, like the trees, like the reflections shimmering in the Seine—severed hands. He closed his eyes, and they became his own again. . . .[11]

From this Sartrean ontology there follows an altogether distinctive theory of values, not to say ethics. It could be superscribed with the general

guiding motto: Value is the anti-viscous. It yields
the following insights.

1. Nausea is the plunge from pure consciousness into the feeling of bodily existence, the con-
glutination of the for-itself with the in-itself. Consciousness begins to slip and, so to speak, slides into
sleep, its tribute to the body, a passing *rigor mortis*;
sleep is the dread which the living body feels of the
future corpse.

2. Under the "look of the other" that turns
man into a rigid object, the intimidated individual
feels his freedom becoming pasty. The other is like
the head of Medusa ("Hell—that is the others!"):
he turns us to stone. The individual, in turn, attempts to petrify the other, by looking back at him;
the result is a fluttering back and forth between
freedom-subject and thing-object, a continuous
change of state.

3. In the face of love's failure to fuse two freedoms into one, sexual desire appears like the swal-
lowing up of consciousness in the quicksand of the
body, the triumph of facts (facticity) over freedom,
of the in-itself over the for-itself.

4. Fortunately, we can escape the vertigo of
this constant fall by a flight into the imagination.
(Kierkegaard, too, felt reflection and fantasy to be
a liberation from the factual world of actual life!)
Art resolutely opposes our hardening in the brute
world of things.

5. But there is a real life in which we must
become engaged; this means that we are prompted

to act freely. Usually, man avoids his freedom, which withdraws before him like running water. The philistine indeed wants to be an object and craves the repose of the stone (seriousness), but does not therefore cease to be free. Freedom curdles like cream. The philistine conglutinates, petrifies into the completed thing, becomes slimy. This is his *mauvaise foi*—his bad conscience.

6. True, genuine existence would be, then, to accept one's freedom despite its evanescent character. We must maintain our freedom within ourselves (this nothingness as a "hole in being"), without getting caught in things. Only such an existence is "authentic," it is the ineluctable precondition of all genuine morality. Thus Sartre's heroes act grossly immoral in the eyes of the philistines—because of their genuine morality. Saint Genêt, the poet-burglar, is the true man who dares to live the free project of his existence. This is a man as man *ought* to be.

Sartre, of course, also describes men as they are: viscous-slimy, fluttering back and forth between freedom and situation, existence and thing—but insofar as they are authentic, they are as nauseated by this existence as is Roquentin and the other heroes of Sartre's novels and plays; Electra, in *The Flies*, is all viscosity, while Orestes is all hope, freeing himself and opposing the sticky sliminess of Jupiter. Orestes, who shakes himself loose from the birdlime of an alien morality and spreads his wings in a new project of existence, appears as Sartre's first moral, authentic character. The people in *The Reprieve* seem to be waiting for the outbreak of war's horrors as if they were waiting for a liberation —the war that will place them into extreme border-line situations and thus make visible the nature of existence: a being-outside-oneself, an existence re-leased from the unfreedom of objects into nothing-ness, into freedom. Existence here is challenged once again to choose itself in free commitment. In *No Exit* we are shown the condition of men who live simultaneously in the *en-soi* and the *pour-soi*: they are dead consciousnesses.

Thus the development of the central ideas of *Being and Nothingness* provides a key to the un-derstanding of Sartre's novels and plays, while these, conversely, present existence by existence, as Plato intended to do in his dialogues, and Kierkegaard in his existential novels by which he overcame "Para-graph 17 of the System." Here, too, we see Sartre's double character, his bastard nature: he needed the two simultaneously, the "Paragraph 17 of the Sys-tem" and his creative works, in order to provide a concrete analysis of existence by means of their mu-tual illumination. The originality of his philos-ophy resides in his unique concretion, reaching the boundlessness of his description of nauseating mat-ter, from which he draws the most abstract conclu-sions. And the other way around: The originality of his literary activity resides in the philosophical penetration of his characters and situations, which, charged with unprecedented symbolic power, concretize, by means of extreme situations, matters such as it had not been possible to present before Sartre. Philosophy and literature, in this typically French synthesis, cannot be understood the one without the other.

4

*Dialogue
with Friend
and Foe*

However ready we may be to follow Sartre's extraordinary lines of thought, it cannot be denied that he frequently loses himself in absolutely untenable regions, images, and scenes. Even the most generous appraisal must admit that Sartre goes too far in using every possible occasion to illustrate philosophical situations by means of the most revolting sexual descriptions whose necessity often remains completely incomprehensible. We cannot rid ourselves of the suspicion, then, that Sartre is in this respect psychopathologically burdened, so that his thought is virtually blocked.

This trend has become more pronounced through the years. His book *Saint Genêt, Actor and Martyr* obviously represents a unique high point in this direction. Earlier books had often repelled even the reader willing to make ample concessions, by their needless crescendo of repulsive excesses. "Existential psychoanalysis" does not, after all, enjoy special license to wallow in Neronian scatology, such as, for example, the sickish sexual experiences of cripples in *The Reprieve*. But when it comes to *Saint Genêt*, his pornographic descriptions of homosexual excesses, of the most revolting violations of the law, and of an anarchic lack of conviction that leaves Stirner's anarchism far behind—all this is beyond discussion. Indeed, there is hardly a book of Sartre's without passages that are bound to provoke the strongest revulsion and objections, totally lacking in all breeding and good taste, whether we think of sexual scenes or other matters.

No wonder, then, that Sartre has many opponents. It is not always easy here to do justice to both
sides. The later his pronouncements, the more bla-
tant are their negative aspects and the more violent
the reactions to them. We need to look carefully in
order to discern what still remains in some measure
justifiable, and what must be ascribed to psycho-
pathological aberrations.

Even Sartre's political pronouncements cannot
be excepted from such scrutiny. At bottom, everything traces back to the bastardization trauma of
his childhood: the hateful reaction of the child assuming himself to be illegitimate, of the precocious
solitary youth who liked to see himself in the dream
role of the *faux bâtard*. Wherever Sartre encounters
illegitimacy—in sexual, economic, aesthetic, scientific, or philosophical matters—he exacerbates and
elaborates the situation to its extremes with a
veritable passion, and draws far-reaching philosophical conclusions by means of deriving everything from masochism and sadism. Let us look once
again at the situation of the *pour-soi/en-soi,*
the for-itself confronting others, since for Sartre every
opposition reveals a traumatic situation:

They see me—no, not even that: *it* sees me. He was the *object*
of looking. A look that searched him to the depths, pierced
him like a knife-thrust, and was not his own look, the embodiment of night . . . condemning him to be himself, coward,
hypocrite, pederast, for all eternity. Himself, quivering beneath that look, and defying it. That look! The night! As if
night was the look. I am *seen.* Transparent, transparent,

transfixed. But by whom? *"I am not alone,"* said Daniel aloud.[1]

Is the other not merely an object, a for-itself to me? Is that body which I see at work anything more to me than a body? What distinguishes the other person from a bodily object is his glance. This glance tells me that the other, too, is a for-itself. Each, we see each other, and the other is just as free as I. "I understand immediately that I am vulnerable, that I take up space and that I can in no case escape from the space where I am defenseless. In short: I am seen," Sartre writes in *Being and Nothingness*. When the other looks at me I tend to feel that I am mere object, *"existant brut"*; I cease to feel free, I am turned to stone. The other is the Gorgo Medusa—in a certain sense I feel myself dying under his look, I have been stolen from myself, my present state has been made eternal, I have assumed the eternal repose of objects, and am set free of my freedom. "Thou lookest at me, and all hope departs; I am weary of my efforts to escape myself. But I know that, beneath thine eye, I *can* no longer escape myself."

I and the other, we are two freedoms which meet, and flee and paralyze each other. We begin to flutter in our existence back and forth between the object-ego and the subject-ego, between ego-object and ego-freedom. The other serves me to grasp myself, otherwise I would be *only* flight. The other's petrifying spectacles keep me imprisoned between object-ego and subject-ego. This is the reason why the other is always my executioner, and I am the executioner of the other, at once both masochist and sadist, fluttering back and forth in the ambivalence of our hate-love. Here we have the basic model of human relations as Sartre sees them.

This constant vacillation between being a subject and being an object, the oscillation between *pour-soi* and *en-soi*, occurs, according to Sartre, throughout nearly all the attempts to solve the subject-object relation that we encounter in the history of philosophy. In personal terms, it is a wavering between shame and *mauvaise foi*, between my body as an *en-soi* and my betrayed freedom as subject in *mauvaise foi*. Hence my viscosity, my sliminess, because I have no center, I have been made headless and do not know what I am about and what I want. Even if we (the other and myself) mutually respect our freedom, we yet cast each other into a world of tolerance and indifference, by mutually condemning each other to freedom and yet remaining incapable of making use of freedom. This is absolute hell, between sadism and masochism (see numerous passages in *Being and Nothingness* and in *The Reprieve*). Thus, Aegisthus exclaims in *The Flies*:

I want that every one of my subjects carry my image within him, and that even in his solitude he feel my severe eye bearing down on his most secret thought. But *I* am their first victim. I see myself any longer only as they seem me, I bend over the open well of their souls, and there is my image, deep down at the bottom. It repels me and fascinates me. Almighty God, who am I other than the fear that the others feel of me? [2]

This is the way things look if Hegel's speculation is to be realized, that my "being for others" is a necessary transition stage in the dialectical development of my "being for myself." (Cf. Kierkegaard's image of Nero.)

Put into practice, Hegel's master-and-slave scheme poisons all human I-and-thou relations and turns them into an I-it bondage. Sartre has now achieved the total perversion of all that is natural. We are no more than mutual enemies in a sexual-pathological battle in which either we or the other must be debased to a thing (*chosiste*). Freedom means either to be subjugated or to subjugate others. Love does not rule, for the sexual craving reveals everything as being ultimately hatred. To be sure, the aberrations of this final phase of our civilization bear Sartre out in many ways. But we only accelerate the rise of the concentration-camp universe if we present this sick distortion of every deviation as the norm, and as ineluctable. Is man indeed so little master of the situation that, with the handwriting on the wall before him, he cannot prevent the inversion of all positive values by making a moral decision—at least in his intention? In Sartre's eyes, apparently, man is not. But then, why this gigantic apparatus of analyses and the assertion: "Existentialism is a humanism"? If I say: Contingency is the Absolute, and resign myself to that, I am no more than a dry leaf in the wind, and all that is human is long since dead—just as God is dead.

The Demolition of Christianity

It was predictable that Sartre would respond to the justified objections of his partners in the dialogue [3] with that same topsy-turvy dialectic that he has demonstrated in philosophy and literature in ever new variations. There is, first, the objection of Christianity, to which Sartre replied by the peculiar position he took, and then again failed to take, with regard to the problem of God. Just as all order is reversed into its opposite, so the original source of order, God, must be radically demolished, and all ethical precepts along with Him. Sartre would rather be debased into an object, by a man, than come to terms with the idea of a supreme cause or an *ens a se*. According to him, man is exclusively an absolute urge for freedom which, however, as we have seen, is nothing else than *spontanéité néantisante* (annihilating spontaneity), directed against himself and the other. The true synthesis between the for-itself and the in-itself could only be God. Thus the real goal of Sartre's man is to become God: "To be man means to reach toward being God. Or if you prefer, man fundamentally is the desire to be God. . . . Human reality is the pure effort to become God, without there being any

given substratum for that effort, without there being *anything* which so endeavors." [4]

But that is a "useles passion"—*"l'homme est
une passion inutile."* The man who wants to be
God for himself and others becomes in practice
nothing but an executioner, for the others and also,
fundamentally, for himself. Closely related is Sartre's argument that man himself has chosen his own
suffering, his own enslavement, and his own executioners. If I merely ponder the question whether it
might not be better to commit suicide, I have already chosen this life and all that it implies.

According to Sartre, it is in the nature of
human consciousness always to be the natural
author of everything. In place of moral responsibility there is now "natural responsibility," just as the
place of God is taken by a "humanistic atheism"
which regards its freedom the ultimate cause of
everything that happens. Nothing that happens can
therefore be subhuman; we ourselves have willed it
so in the free struggle for existence. In every single
engagement, we dispose not only of ourselves, but
also of all humanity and the whole universe. This
view leads to the total atomization of knowledge,
values, human society; it leads to chaos, Hobbes'
war of all against all, just as the teachings of the
sophists would have done; they would have meant
the end of philosophy and of human society, had
there not been a Socrates to stake his life on a uni-
versally valid truth which every man can find in his

own heart. Here the genuinely existential thought of Socrates opposes Sartre's existentialism.

Christian Opposition

Thus it is worth our while to listen when the views of Christian thinkers who, after Socrates, were the first existentialist thinkers—men like St. Paul, Augustine, Luther, Pascal, Kierkegaard—are presented in opposition to Sartre. The Christian existentialist Gabriel Marcel in part gives expression to this thinking. To the mere for-itself and in-itself he opposes the attitude of the genuine I-Thou relation whose arch-model is the relation of man to God, in prayer; in the place of the *not*, he puts the affirmation that knows its source to be God, and that against a background of unbelief posits faith; against a background of hate, love; against a background of treason, loyalty, the readiness for onto-logical permanence.

The negative aspects must be taken seriously for the sake of the positive ones, just as the serious choice of life can be made only against the back-ground of the temptation to commit suicide. But Marcel points out that Sartre merely "describes," that he is concerned solely with things, *"chosiste"* (a thing-like It), and thus gets stranded in agnosti-cism. Sartre's forever uncompleted man is funda-mentally envious of the in-itself of things, and identifies himself with it. He is a constant lack of

content defining himself as nothingness, Marcel
says. Thus Sartre would practically have come close
to the position of purely materialistic philosophers
like Felix Le Dantec, for whom consciousness is
merely a physiological epiphenomenon. For them,
too, Marcel goes on, consciousness is a useless chem-
ical emanation. Sartre, by mixing freedom into
everything, devalues it and makes it the object of a
pre-established hierarchy. A freedom "to which I
am condemned" is not freedom but its distorted
counterpart: This necessity to choose ("free to
choose, but not free *not* to choose") is merely a
form of contingency, Sartre's *condition humaine* is
a false freedom, not freedom in its essential nature.
His inter-human relations are nothing else but
rivalries and battles, "transcended transcendences."
It would seem to us that, against Sartre, it must be
pointed out further that freedom lies in the free
decision concerning our relation to divine transcendence.

In his *Existentialism*, his dialogue with his opponents, Sartre merely ridiculed the Christian objections, and brushed them aside with dialectical
trickery. But fundamentally, he plays fast and loose
only with his own atheism, as is illustrated in his
play, *The Devil and the Good Lord*. On the occasion of that play's first performance, he said to Professor Jean Guitton in an interview:

In my opinion, the ideologies confronting each other today
put in question our whole image of man and our transcendence. I believe that the Reformation thesis—which we en-

counter among almost all of Luther's opponents no less than in Luther himself—according to which every man is a prophet, is far more enlightening than the thesis of the French Revolution, according to which all men are born equal. This thesis of an absolute religious value that every man has for all men prompted me to prefer the Reformation, and especially the peasant prophets of those days, to all other historical situations and figures. . . . Universalist atheism is not time-bound, it is the purely abstract and unhistorical assertion that God is not. The mistake of that ideology is not that it denies God's existence, but that it fails to notice that we today still belong to a religious form of culture in which the vast majority of people are believers, or at least half-believers. This is why I invoke Nietzsche's "God is dead." We are still under the influence of Christianity. We still have to absorb a number of things which, incidentally, we encounter also in Marxist thought. What shall I say about Marxism? It is unhistorical, hence unfruitful (!) . As unfruitful as would be the position of an internationalist who—desirous to be a citizen of the world—failed to note that we are moving toward an exacerbation of national feelings. Atheism has to be re-examined.

To this day, Sartre has failed to give us that re-examination, as well as that "ethics" which he promised toward the end of this interview; considering his dialectical presuppositions, he would seem unable to make those promises good.

The Quarrel with Camus

Matters are similar when we come to his confrontation with true humanism, as personified by the poet Camus: from the start, and even after the occupation had ended, the two were comrades in arms. Sartre was, at that time, leader of a political group, *Rassemblement Démocratique Républicaine*, which intended to reach across all parties and be an *anti*-revolutionary movement. It championed the concrete freedom of the individual, especially the workingman, which, so the movement claimed, had been surrendered even by the communists! Sartre and Camus also had in common a number of slogans and technical terms, such as the concept of the absurd, and their restriction to immanence without any transcendental perspective. But it is only at first glance that many points of the two views appear to coincide.

How radically the atheism and even the humanism of Camus differ from those of Sartre can be seen in the famous *Querelle Sartre-Camus*, which in August of 1952 terminated the friendship of the two men. According to Camus, there is no such thing as a free project of existence, but rather freedom itself is what is absurd. In the two thought systems of these two thinkers, the absurd is refracted by totally different media. They represent radically different types of mind. Sartre is all intellect, and proposes the extreme perversion of all that has so far been thought valid. Camus is poetically and intuitively more profound, more deliberate; he destroys nothing merely for the sake of destruction, and grants to others their freedom, as a true humanist. After making due allowances, it may be said that Sartre stands to Camus as Descartes stands to St. Augustine, who saw man in his totality as an integral being.

Camus' position with regard to God, to history and metahistory, and to the values of humanism, was infinitely more profound, more tentative, and more responsible than Sartre's. Fundamentally, he even took the absurd far more serious than Sartre, because he took the double character of human existence, between immanence and transcendence, more seriously; the tensions in Camus' thought were far more fruitful and far greater. In his brilliantly polished farewell letter (in *Temps Modernes* of August, 1952, a reply to Camus' complaint about a negative review of his *Man in Revolt*), Sartre attacked Camus: Where did Camus get his humanistic values, when every ethic was to be rejected? Camus was asocial, since he asserted that all the revolts since 1789 had done nothing but put man in God's place! Camus was not a champion and helper of the oppressed, he did not want to commit himself in action, he always wanted to keep his hands clean!

Camus, however, took the absurd seriously; thus he could not run after the prophets of his day, large and small, as Sartre did again and again in a wild criss-cross chase, only to regret it later. Sartre, too, says in *Situations: Nous parlons dans le désert* —we are speaking in the wilderness, and at bottom he knows that no party satisfies him. To Sartre's accusation that Camus did not totally surrender to facticity and historism, Camus replied that man could not, to be sure, live without history, but that he must not idolize it panlogistically in Hegel's sense and must not become submerged in pan-historism; man must, at the same time, take a metahistorical position and realize that nature and history merely serve to illustrate man's situation in the tension of the absurd. Camus stated his viewpoint with precision in *Man in Revolt*:

This book does not deny history, but on the contrary proposes to show that pure anti-historism, at least today, is just as destructive as pure historism. For those who know how to read my work I have written here that people who believe in history only are on their way toward terror, while those who do not believe in history at all authorize that terror.

Sartre, Camus asserted, had "called one thousand advocates into the field, but not one brother." Sartre, he went on, and his likes sit in their well-heated editorial offices and by their total silence condemn to death the most miserable victims of today's revolutionary terror, because these people are in their way politically. The misery of those oppressed by the Marxist revolution, Camus claimed, could possibly be justified with a view to a future good. But if, as Sartre held, even man makes no sense, how could he ascribe any sense and meaning to history—a sense and meaning discernible even now? The existentialist would be threatened at his very foundations if he were to admit that history had any foreseeable meaning. But if he did not want to make that admission, Camus continued, then his attitude was merely frivolous and cruel.

He robbed man of every reason to fight for meaningful objectives, in order to throw him into a party. Boundless freedom becomes boundless slavery. Sartre's existentialism was itself a denial of the sole consolation of the victims of revolution: that they were being sacrificed to some future happiness. Ultimately, Camus concluded, Sartre's position was pure nihilism. "One cannot move about in history if one does not believe in values!" And to Sartre's headlong plunge from nihilism into communism, Camus opposed this insight: "We shall not do battle against the shameless masters of our era by making fine distinctions among their slaves!"

Neo-Marxism, or the "Bastard" Seeks a Home

This brings us to the point where we must give closer attention to Sartre's curious attitude toward communism. We earlier noted his remark that "Marxism is unhistorical, hence unfruitful," and his complaint that he was living in a desert. Nonetheless it seems that his executioner-victim-gas-chamber psychology has left Sartre with masochistically perverted tendencies that prompt him to steer a curious zig-zag course. (We think here of the Vienna Peace Congress, the protest about Hungary, etc.) The number of accusations that the Communist Party has raised against Sartre is legion, and if he had been a member he would hardly have remained in the party for a year before being excluded because of deviations. These are some ex-

amples of Marxist criticism: Sartre is "a writer who
has made the wrong commitment" or a "philosopher of the fear of revolution," a being who is imprisoned in capitalist contradictions, a putrefied
intellectual and Johnny-come-lately of bourgeois
decadence, the typical leader who is a failure in
contemporary society; his work deals only with obsolete problems that lack all interest, they are "an
attempt that is doomed to failure." H. Mougin wrote
a whole book, modeled on Marx's "Holy Family,"
under the title *La sainte famille existentialiste,*
which convicted Sartre of every mistake he had by
then committed. Many of the accusations coincide
almost verbatim with those of the other side: sub-
jectivist, individualist, conscientialist, irrationalist,
nihilist, anarchist. Sartre, they claim, is torn between the desire for absolute freedom and a deci-
sionistic decision-making for the sake of commitment alone.

The youthful trauma of his fear of bastardization, his lack of property, his flirtation with the
sudden discovery that he, as an illegitimate child,
was one of the disinherited, inclined him early
toward proletarian sympathies. The position of the
"salauds" (slobs) who take shelter behind their al-
leged "right"—a pretense that allows the executioners to torture their victims—all the elements of
a puberty revolt of the protected young bourgeois
from a good family: all this predisposed Sartre to
that inconsistency with which he again and again
deserted his position of absolute freedom, only to

withdraw again, disappointed, into his "desert," the desert of totally unprincipled anarchism, unbridled sexuality, and the exaltation of crime and torture. It is not quite comprehensible why Sartre took part in the resistance, since he considered the *"univers concentrationaire"* normal for our age. In any event, he might look up what, Lukacz, for example, in his *Demolition of Reason*, had to say about him and his philosophy as the product of the decay of bourgeois-capitalist decadence in its final stage.

Sartre's scientific position with regard to dialectical materialism shows a highly personal dialectic peculiar to him alone, which we must trace here in greater detail. In the first part of his essay "Materialism and Revolution," where he constantly pits one Marxist thinker against another (for instance, Engels against Marx), Sartre does away completely with the scientific validity of the Marxist idea of matter. He attacks the Marxist concept of causality: "The materialists' cause can find no support in science, nor can it get any comfort from dialectics; it remains a crude and purely practical concept, a symptom of the constant effort of materialism to distort the one in the direction of the other, and to join by force two methods which exclude each other. It is the archetype of the false synthesis, and the use that is being made of it is dishonest."

In a like manner, the dialectic of dialectical

materialism is a secret borrowing from idealism: "It must indeed be recognized that materialism, by pretending to be dialectical, 'leads over' into idealism. The Marxists claim to be positivists, and destroy their positivism by the use they make, implicitly, of metaphysics; they proclaim their rationalism and in the same breath demolish it by their view of the genesis of thinking: and in the same fashion they deny their own principle—which is materialism—at the very moment when they establish it, by a secret recourse to idealism." A consciousness that precedes being (which is the very opposite of materialism) is the only dialectical consciousness, Sartre holds.

The Hegelian consciousness did not need to *establish* a dialectical *hypothesis*. It is not merely an objective witness who stands by on the outside when ideas are being procreated: it is itself dialectical, it procreates itself according to the laws of synthetic progression; there is no need for it to *assume* necessity within relations—it *is* this necessity, lives it. And it has this certainty not by virtue of some evidence which is more or less subject to criticism, but by virtue of the progressive identification of the dialectic of consciousness with the consciousness of dialectic. If, on the contrary, dialectic represents the manner in which the material world evolves; if consciousness, far from being wholly identified with dialectic, is merely a "mirror image of being," a partial product, a moment of synthetic progression; if consciousness, instead of sharing from within in its own creation, is merely assailed from outside by feelings and ideologies which are rooted outside consciousness and which consciousness must suffer without creating them: if that is so, then consciousness is merely a link in a chain whose beginning and end lie very far apart;

and then, since it is not the whole chain, can it make any *definite* statement about the chain? [5]

But Sartre is not ready to make the *sacrificium intellectus* to materialism.[6]

"Get down on your knees, and you will believe," says Pascal. The materialist's undertaking comes very close to that. If the issue were that I alone must get down on my knees in order to assure the happiness of mankind, there is no doubt that I would agree. But the issue is to renounce everybody's right to free criticism, to evidence, and ultimately to truth. I have been told that all these will be given back to us later; but I have no proof: and how can I believe in a promise made in the name of principles that are self-destructive? I only know one thing: that *today* I must not cut off my thinking. Have I landed in the unacceptable dilemma, that I must betray the cause of the proletariate in the name of truth, or betray truth in order to serve the proletariate? [7]

Still, Sartre is prepared to let Marxism stand as a faith, a myth of action—though not as a science. And now, in the second part of his essay, he looks on the whole matter again in terms of the subject-object-dilemma of in-itself and for-itself:

It can no doubt be said that the result of materialism is to lure the master into the trap, and make him into a thing just like the slave. But the man in command knows nothing about it, and does not care: he lives in the lap of his ideologies, his rights, and his culture. *Only* to the slaves' subjectivity does he appear as a thing. Therefore, it is infinitely more right and useful to let the slave discover, through his labor, his freedom to change the world and thus his own condition, than it is to strain all our powers in order to show the slave that the master is a thing—which means to conceal his own true power from the slave. And if it is true that materialism, the explanation of the higher in terms of the lower, is indeed a fitting picture of the present structure of our society, then it is all the more obvious that materialism is a mere myth, in the Platonic sense of the word. For the revolutionary has no use for a symbolic explanation of the present situation; what he needs is an idea that allows him to forge the future. The materialist myth, however, is bound to lose all meaning in a classless society in which there will no longer be any higher and lower men.[8]

And although Sartre endorses the *élan* of revolution, he feels compelled to doubt its theoretical foundation, and closes with this exclamation:

For the communists are stuck, caught between the fact that the materialistic myth has become decrepit, and the fear of a split or at least indecision in their ranks if they adopt a new ideology. The best minds among them remain silent; the silence is filled with the chatter of their dolts. . . . One cannot with impunity shape an entire generation by teaching them successful errors. What will happen on that day when materialism chokes the revolutionary project?

A Kant of Marxist Philosophy?

In Sartre's *Critique de la raison dialectique* (1960), there are similar instances of a self-willed criticism deviating from the party line that are all the more noteworthy because Sartre had tried again and again to adapt himself to the concrete expressions of revolutionary theory. Here, too, he starts with the assumption that consciousness is something primary, internal, spiritual, and not a mere emanation of being, of matter, of man's biological and social structure. In the introduction he admits his conviction that historical materialism furnishes the only valid interpretation of history, and at the same time that existentialism represents the only concrete approximation to reality. With this *"at the same time,"* which he himself emphasizes, he indicates the profound dilemma in which he has found himself caught for the last fifteen years: convinced that his own starting point was the only one scientifically possible; convinced at the same time, however, that communism with its revolutionary interpretation of history was the only right approach for revolutionary practice; and unable at the same time to admit the theoretical validity of the starting point of dialectical materialism. In the introductory chapter, "Search for a Method," he states outright that communist thought has become "sclerotic" in its present phase, calcified within a compulsive doctrine, and has forgotten to dust off its own sources. "After communism had transformed us, and had eliminated for us the categories of bourgeois thought, it failed to satisfy our need to *understand* in that special position into which we had been placed. It had no longer anything new to teach us because it had stopped dead."

But Sartre continues to *believe* that this political direction is the only effective way in history. Its truth, however, is *practical*-empirical. But its philosophical foundations are shaky. He asks: Why are we not Marxists? And he answers: Because the assertions of Engels and others are mere guidelines for practical undertakings but do not offer concrete truths. Marxism does not make mistakes in action, but its philosophy has stopped developing further. Sartre, accordingly, would wish to make a suggestion concerning the self-criticism that is necessary. So far, Marxist philosophy had been held captive within dogmatism.

Sartre's *Critique de la raison dialectique* [Critique of Dialectical Reason] is an attempt to provide the further development needed. What Kant had done for epistemology (Sartre accepts, for instance, Kant's categorical imperative), Sartre would do for Marxist philosophy. The thinking of dialectical materialism is an empirical anthropology. Sartre would have it absorb the disciplines which until now had remained outside it. These disciplines include essentially a phenomenology of the structures of existence, dealing primarily with the facts of consciousness, not the social facts.

Thus, in a manner of speaking, Sartre again turns Marxism upside down. Being does not determine consciousness; consciousness determines being. He rejects the biological and social starting point of Marxism, and starts from the individual, from consciousness, even though the individual in its present social position is almost extinguished: "We refuse absolutely to mistake suppressed man for an object, and to mistake his alienation for the physical laws that rule contingency. We assert the special nature of human action, which breaks out of the social milieu even though that milieu remains wholly determined in the process. . . ." [10]

Man, however, is not simply the result of his being materially determined. Man is the project *(projet)* of an action—men are projects that in their consciousness carry out an individual or a group within this determined setting.

Once again, we encounter Sartre's theory of freedom and responsibility. Hegel's progression of history which, as Hegel grew old, ossified into a closed dialectic in Prussian officialdom, had been loosened up again and changed into an open dialectic by Marx and Engels, who turned Hegel's thought "inside out." Sartre, in his turn, believes that he must now loosen up the ossified closed dialectic of aging Marxism by his critical objections and his dialectic of consciousness; he must start with the individual, because we come into the world as individuals and leave it again as individuals who have been profoundly shaken and shocked by the forced collectivism of the concentration-camp era that is the present.

Sartre here attempts a synthesis of his own Marxist philosophy, but he must start with the living experience of the individual. In this critique of dialectical reason, Marxist dialectic ceases to be a social mechanism, "so that it may be lived by the individual." Naturally, it will not be lived in individualistic solitude. Sartre had demonstrated earlier that every individual, despite all his freedom and autonomy, is imbedded in a situation which determines him, but which the individual may either accept, or transform, or breach. His aim in the *Cri-*

tique de la raison dialectique to show that living individual experience is not merely a reflex of social
conditions (as it is in dialectical materialism), but
the living, concrete aspect of the statistical facts. The
statistical, amorphous object-character, to which
Sartre had earlier objected so passionately, is erased
only by the concrete life of the individual consciousness, through which the subject turns from an in-
itself into a for-itself. The problem of synthesizing
these two modes of thought Sartre calls *"totalisa-
tion"*:[11] it is the transition from the individual to
the collective, from individual consciousness to history. What is the process by which the individual
experiences "totalize" themselves into the collective phenomenon of Marxism? "For us, the problem is one of connecting the two. If there are individuals, *who* totalizes *what*?" Sartre, in order to
find the answer, transfers the "dialectical movement" from the group to the individual (that is, in
the direction opposite to that of Marxism). He considers consciousness the source of the collective, not
the other way around. The individual is the one to
experience social reality, to react, to develop dialectically, and thus to create the social dialectic.
"All historical dialectic rests upon individual practice, in that this individual practice is itself already
dialectical." The movement of history thus issues
from the individuals, not in any magical or statistical manner but because the individuals themselves, in the normal dialectic of their lives, show

the need of totalization which produces collective phenomena.

Sartre now sets out to study the movement that leads to history, beginning with the dawn of consciousness in the individual. The work's first large section thus is entitled "From Individual Practice to the Practical-Inert," meaning economic practice as the basis of Marxism—"Inert" because it is not yet historic action. This transition is shown in the second main part, "From the Group of History." A second volume has been promised to complete the picture of *Critique de la raison dialectique*. Freedom and necessity are to be united. (Marx: "Freedom is the insight into necessity.") In every stage of his development, the individual produces a social totalization, which assumes historical meaning in the confrontation of freedom and necessity by transcending its situation. "Freedom and necessity are only one. . . . It is an individual construction whose single factors are the individual human beings as free activities." Thus Sartre thinks to supply Marxism with a foundation of human freedom. Could this be, fundamentally, also the explication of his theory that everything, even the most frightful horrors, are freely willed by man: "There is no such thing as inhuman situation"?

His boundless yearning for freedom, with which he started in 1938, led Sartre to the void that frightened him and that he wanted to fill with responsibility; and from individual responsibility he has now progressed to social and from there to his-

torical responsibility, the historical responsibility
of his headstrong neo-Marxism (yet Sartre does not,
at bottom, believe in progress [12]) which it is highly
doubtful will ever receive official approval. All this
he did precisely because he started at the opposite
end, with the individual, mind, consciousness (and
that in the sense of existential psychoanalysis!). Can
there be any other answer than that which Garaudy,
one of the official philosophers of French Marxism,
gave to Sartre as early as 1946: "Sartre rejects materialism and claims nonetheless that he avoids
idealism. Here stands the revealed the nullity of
this impossible 'Third Party' . . ."? Is Sartre not
bound to reap bitter experiences from this zig-zag
way of his? Just as no man can maintain himself
in a radical skepticism, which must of necessity turn
into blind fideism, just so Sartre will have to make
a turnabout from the absolute freedom of nothingness into a blind subjection to a firm, massive doctrine. Thus he even says that his philosophy is nothing else than an enclave within Marxism, even
though his argumentation is totally un-Marxist
since his starting point is the individual, the unique
personality and his consciousness. Even if we cannot share his viewpoint, we would remind those
who blame Sartre for having such political inclinations at all that political inclinations, too, must be
left to the free decision of an individual thinker
who strives so hard and at such length to find
grounds for his position—and this even if again and
again he makes presuppositions that seem emotion-

who says this?

al rather than rational. We will have to wait before we can know whether the homeless, estranged existentialist finds a home for his philosophy in the "rich earth of Marxism," as he put it, or whether he arrives at the same conclusion as did his abandoned, now dead, friend Camus: "The revolution, even that and especially that which claims to be the materialistic revolution, is nothing but an unbridled metaphysical crusade."

5

❖❖❖❖❖❖❖❖❖❖❖❖❖❖❖❖❖❖❖❖❖❖❖❖❖❖❖❖❖❖

Liquidation
of the Past—
Not a Faith
for the Future

In closing, we might ask ourselves what view we should take of Sartre, as a thinker and a creative writer. The answer lies perhaps in what Jaspers once said about thinkers such as Nietzsche: They are liquidators of the past—but their truth becomes inverted into its total opposite if we succumb to their fascination and accept as regulative what can be valid only as a corrective. What Jaspers urges on the readers of Nietzsche holds equally true for Sartre's readers:

This thinking calls for a high degree of freedom in man, but not an empty freedom which has merely cast off everything, but a fulfilled freedom which, incomprehensible to man, comes to his encounter out of man's historic depth. Whoever allows himself to be seduced by Nietzsche into the sophistry of mere propositions, the sheer semblance of understanding gained, intoxication with the extreme, the capriciousness of instinct—such a reader is accursed by Nietzsche from the outset.[1]

Sartre is an original thinker, literary creator, and poetic craftsman when it comes to showing up and clarifying the symptoms of stagnation in our time. To carry out this function, the unhappy disposition with which his youthful trauma of bastardization left him was no doubt necessary and meaningful, because by exacerbating the phenomena he managed to arouse his contemporaries. As a training academy in the acrobatics of a life-related dialectic, too, he may serve as a stimulating and invigorating transition stage. But if we want to stop with him, and allow ourselves to be dazzled by his fascination, then all the good that he could do us turns into the exact opposite. Sartre is the liquidator of all false stagnation—but the attempt to provide positive solutions must be made by the reader himself; just as the reader is left to his own devices to decide how much of Sartre is mere sophistical revolt and how much genuine philosophizing, or what is no more than a psycho-pathological prejudice of the puberty spite of *épater le bourgeois,* and what the true presentation of a problem. The attitude with which we must approach Sartre is— Socratic irony.

Thus our detour through the most extreme existentialism leads us back to the genuinely existentialist thinkers, whose substance has been borrowed by all the schools of modern philosophy of existence: Socrates, St. Paul, Augustine, Luther, Pascal, Kierkegaard. Sartre, by contrast, represents a retrogression to the lowest level of the aesthetic stage of existence, which wins its struggle for meaning and fulfillment only in the ethical stage, and in fact only in the "religiousness B" of the religious stage; a personal and authentic religiosity in the original experience of the tensions which are produced by the paradox that earthly immanence and divine transcendence are present simultaneously in man's individual existence. Sartre presents only the most extreme consequences of an existence *without* all transcendence, an existence that was shipwrecked upon the cliffs of the aesthetic stage, despair [2], while the existential thinkers discard justification on the strength of our own intellectual powers, and set in its place genuine justification of our existence through transcendence.

Sartre can at best muster a premature, half skeptical-dialectical "faith" in this world stripped of all transcendence, a faith which is ever anew disappointed; and thus he lacks precisely the one category that can spring only from the paradox of a genuine faith (faith as an opening of one's own spirit toward the unknown future); he lacks the category which Kierkegaard called the single most important one for modern man—the *"repetition* as a memory pointing forward." Even Camus, poet of alienation and the absurd, still found it possible to allow this category in his *Myth of Sisyphus*. Thus there is only one thing left of Sartre's philosophical and literary work: a merciless dialectic—with ever new dramatic, epic, and philosophical facets, highly polished and yet always charged with emotion— which, though (perhaps pathologically) distorted, serves to disrupt and destroy structures of every kind that have grown rigid in convention, and are thereby inescapably pointed toward the past.[3]

Up to this point we have discovered that Sartre is capable of shattering things in the most diverse and imaginative ways; but what structures will arise in future in the dismantled spaces is for the time being an entirely open question. With his secularization (*laicization*) of the absolute, and with the transformation of eschatological, eternal goals into the purely immanent worldliness of earthly goals, Sartre may have permanently blocked his own way to the openness of faith toward an unknown future. But it must be regarded as a positive result that Sartre—like the other great liquidators of the past—has carried through a new project of existence toward the future. He may have done no more than show, once and for all, that this project is an error; but there is now no longer an escape back into a conformist past: from now on we must think our way through Sartre toward the new that is to come.

Chronology

When a French title has been translated into English, the title of the English edition is given within parentheses following the original title.

1905:   Born June 21 in Paris.
1907:   Death of father: return to home of paternal grandfather, Charles Schweitzer, in Alsace.
1916:   Remarriage of mother; move to La Rochelle.
1924:   Graduated from Lycée Henri IV in Paris.
1924–28: Studied at École Normale Supérieure.
1928:   Beginning of friendship with Simone de Beauvoir.
1929:   Won first place in competitive examination for the Agrégation de Philosophie, having failed the previous year.
1931–33: Taught philosophy in the *lycée* at Le Havre.
1933–34: Studied with Husserl and Heidegger in Berlin.
1934–39: Taught philosophy in *lycées* at Le Havre, Laon, and Paris.
1936:   Published *La Transcendance de l'égo* (The Transcendence of the Ego) and *L'Imagination*.
1938:   Published *La Nausée* (Nausea).
1939:   Published *Le Mur* (The Wall) and *Esquisse d'une théorie des émotions* (The Emotion: Outline of a Theory). Mobilized at outbreak of World War II.

1940:   Published *L'Imaginaire, psychologie phénoménolo-
        gique de l'imagination* (Psychology of Imagination) .
        Taken prisoner by the Germans.

1941:   Released from prisoner-of-war camp.

1941–45:   Taught in Paris.

1942:   Met Albert Camus in Paris.

1943:   Published *L'Etre et le néant* (Being and Nothing-
        ness), *Les Mouches* (The Flies) *Explication de
        l'étranger* (collected in *Situations I*) .

1943–44:   Active in French resistance.

1944:   Published *Huis Clos* (No Exit) .

1945:   Founded periodical *Les Temps Modernes.* Published
        Les Chemins de la liberté, I: *L'Age de raison* (Age of
        Reason) , II: *Le Sursis* (The Reprieve) . Made trip to
        U.S.A.

1946:   Published *Morts sans sépulture,* (The Victors) *La
        Putain respectueuse* (The Respectful Prostitute),
        L'Existentialisme est un humanisme, and *Réflexions
        sur la question juive.*

1947:   Published *Baudelaire, Situations I* (early critical ar-
        ticles), *Les Jeux sont faits* (The Chips Are Down)
        and *Qu'est-ce que la littérature* (What Is Literature)
        (in *Situations II*) .

1948:   Published *Les Mains sales* (Dirty Hands), *L'Engre-
        nage* (In the Mesh) , and *Situations II.* Founded with
        David Rousset, Gerard Rosenthal and others the
        non-Communist leftist political party Le Rassemble-
        ment Démocratique Révolutionnaire, disbanded late
        in 1949.

1949:   Published *Les Chemins de la liberté,* III: *La Mort
        dans l'âme* (Troubled Sleep) and *Situations III*
        (articles on French resistance, U.S.A., literary and art
        criticism).

1951:   Published *Le Diable et le bon Dieu* (The Devil and
        the Good Lord) .

1952:   Published *Saint Genêt, comedien et martyr.* (Saint

Genêt, Actor and Martyr). Broke with Camus over latter's *L'Homme révolté*. Published *Les Communistes et la paix* (in *Situations VI*) indicating close collaboration with Communist Party.

1953: Published (with others) *L'Affaire Henri Martin*, defending sailor arrested for opposition to Indo-Chinese war.

1954: Published *Kean* (adapted from Dumas).

1956: Published *Nekrassov*. Broke with Communists over Stalinist repression in Hungary. Published *Le Fantôme de Staline* (in *Situations VII*).

1957: Published *Questions de méthode*.

1960: Published *Critique de la raison dialectique* and *Les Séquestrés d'Altona* (The Condemned of Altona). Was first to sign "Déclaration des 121," manifesto against atrocities in Algeria. Visited Cuba.

1961: Second visit to Cuba. His favorable reactions published here as *Sartre on Cuba*.

1963: Published *Les Mots*.

1964: Published *Situations IV. Portraits. Situations V. Colonialisme et Néo-Colonialisme. Situations VI. Problèmes du Marxisme, 1*. Was awarded Nobel Prize for Literature, but rejected it.

1965: Published: *Les Troyennes* (adapted from Aeschylus); *Situations VII. Problèmes du Marxisme, 2. Que peut la littérature?* (with others).

1966: Published *Flaubert* in *Les Temps Modernes*.

1967: Participated in International War Crimes Tribunal in Stockholm and Copenhagen. Wrote *Le Génocide*, section of final report condemning American policy in Vietnam.

1968: Publicly condemned Russian invasion of Czechoslovakia.

1969: Publicly condemned purported American atrocities at My Lai and Songmy in Vietnam.

Notes

1 Alienation and Justification: Roots of Creativity

1. *Nausea,* tr. Lloyd Alexander (New York: New Directions, 1949), p. 238.
2. Article in *Action,* December 29, 1944.
3. Article in *Action,* December 29, 1944.

2 The Principal Themes of Sartre's Thought

1. *Being and Nothingness,* tr. Hazel E. Barnes (New York: Philosophical Library, 1956), p. 626.
2. *Being and Nothingness,* p. 615.
3. Rom. 7:19.
4. *The Transcendence of the Ego,* tr. Forrest Williams and Robert Kirkpatrick (New York: Noonday Press, 1957).
5. *Ideas,* para. 23.
6. *Imagination,* tr. Forrest Williams (Ann Arbor: University of Michigan Press, 1962), p. 134.

7. Vol. 52, January, 1939.
8. *The Psychology of Imagination* (New York: Philosophical Library, 1948), p. 177.
9. *Nausea,* p. 234.
10. *Nausea,* p. 233.
11. *Théorie des emotions,* p. 35.
12. In *The Wall and Other Stories,* tr. Lloyd Alexander (New York: New Directions, 1948), p. 63.
13. In *The Wall and Other Stories,* pp. 67–68.
14. In *The Wall and Other Stories,* p. 77.
15. *The Psychology of Imagination,* p. 214.
16. Pp. 596–97.
17. *The Psychology of Imagination,* p. 103.
18. *Nausea,* pp. 170–71.
19. *Nausea,* pp. 173–74.
20. The old Lutheran problem of *justification* by faith has here been unexpectedly resurrected, wholly secularized, in pure immanence. Is this Sartre's unconscious inheritance from his theological forebears? This totally secularized renewal of a central religious theme originally intended as transcendental holds the root of Sartre's genuine concern, but also of the basically tragic aberrations of his existential analysis of existence. Similar suggestions can be found in Heidegger—but there they end up in the mystique of Being of his last phase. (L.R.)
21. *Nausea,* p. 176.
22. *Nausea,* pp. 176–77.

3   *Resistance: Freedom and Responsibility*

1. "Republic of Silence" in *Lettres françaises,* 1944.
2. "Republic of Silence."
3. *Being and Nothingness,* p. 11.
4. Heidegger, *What Is Metaphysics?*

5. *What Is Metaphysics?* pp. 39–40.
6. *The Psychology of Imagination,* p. 266.
7. *Being and Nothingness,* p. lxviii.
8. *The Reprieve,* tr. Eric Sutton (New York: Alfred A. Knopf, 1951), p. 62.
9. *The Reprieve,* pp. 362–63.
10. *The Reprieve,* pp. 362–63.
11. *The Reprieve,* p. 363.

4   Dialogue with Friend and Foe

1. *The Reprieve,* pp. 135–36.
2. *The Flies.* From the French, by translator.
3. We lack the space here to deal with the numerous polemics of the various schools of philosophical thought in France, such as that of the Cartesians (Alquié) and others. (L.R.)
4. *Being and Nothingness,* pp. 566 and 576.
5. "Materialism and Revolution." From the French, by translator.
6. Both his *Existentialism* and his "Materialism and Revolution" show that Sartre never ceased arguing these questions seriously with the official representatives of the French Communist Party—though unsuccessfully! (L.R.)
7. "Materialism and Revolution." From the French, by translator.
8. *Ibid.*
9. *Ibid.*
10. *Critique de la raison dialectique.* From the French, by translator.
11. See *Critique de la raison dialectique,* and see also Sartre's *What Is Literature?,* tr. Bernard Frechtman (New York, Philosophical Library, 1949).
12. "It is true that we do not believe in progress; prog-

ress is an improvement; man is always the same in the face of a situation which changes, and his choice always remains a choice within a situation."

5   *Liquidation of the Past—Not a Faith for the Future*

1. *Nietzsche and Christianity,* 1952, p. 70.
2. Kierkegaard, in his *Sickness Unto Death,* has shown that this despair is a *necessary* transitional stage for modern man.
3. Compare Roquentin's remark: "I might succeed—in the past, nothing but the past—in accepting myself." (*Nausea,* p. 238)